AWAKENING HAIR
Caring for Your Cosmic Antenna

Laura Sullivan & Linda Deslauriers

SUNDREAM ॐ PUBLISHING

Sundream Publishing
www.sundreampublishing.com

Printed in the United States of America

ISBN-10: 1944669000
ISBN-13: 978-1944669003

For William Mercury Yount

1948 - 1990

CONTENTS

Introduction   7

Ever Present Nature   12

Our Hair - Roots and Antennae   14

The Power of Hair Gardening   18

The Yin and Yang of Hair Care   30

What Kind of Hair Do You Have?   33

Discover Your Hair Care Style   41

Nature's Elements for Your Hair   45

Your Hair Care Improvement Plan   109

Sun and Moon Cycles and Your Hair   114

Five Easy Steps to Sustainable Hair Care   123

Hair in the Light   128

Ingredient Alert Guide   132

About Us   135

Acknowledgements   143

Look deep into nature, and then you will
understand everything better.

Albert Einstein

INTRODUCTION

The Essence of Hair

Hair is a powerful part of us.
Hair is part of our body, mind, and soul.
Hair is history and time. Hair is culture.
Hair is an expression of the self,
and hair is simply hair.
Hair touches the lives of others.
Hair is an essential part of life.

Welcome to Awakening Hair, a transformational journey to a happier, healthier, and more conscious experience with your hair. Knowledge of the most effective and life-enhancing practices, products, and insights from our work with thousands of people's hair may help you to realize your best hair ever.

- ♥ You can significantly improve the quality and beauty of your hair without resorting to harmful chemicals.
- ♥ It is possible to have a deeply appreciative and supportive relationship with your hair, which can translate into having the hair of your dreams.
- ♥ You can be in harmony with your hair, feeling beautiful, confident, and free.

When it comes to hair, following nature's guidance creates the best results. Aligning with nature, integrating the gifts of its elements and rhythms sustains your hair's health, bringing out its true magnificence.

We will start at the 'root,' understanding the basic functions and properties of the different kinds of hair that we, as humans, have. The best way to experience hair freedom, meaning your hair is healthy, easy to care for, and beautiful, is first to understand hair, and then to understand YOUR hair.

Hair is connected to life in fundamental, profound, and even magical ways. The hair growth cycle, in essence, symbolizes the larger life cycle. Each single hair grows, rests, falls out, and a new one grows in its place. Birth, life, death, and then new birth, new life, and transition take place again and again.

The head and hair are the first parts of our body to go through the birth canal into a completely new environment, to be witnessed and touched by another human being. It is generally the first characteristic to receive attention and people continue to comment on our hair throughout our lives. It is as if our hair becomes public domain. Our hair grows and evolves with us, documenting our different life phases and cultural influences. Hair is the flag each generation flies to identify its own sense of beauty, ideals, and aspirations.

Hair tells as many tales as there are people on this globe. It is woven into rituals and customs creating unique and universal patterns throughout the world. Hair is our cosmic antenna. Before you are close enough to make eye contact or shake hands, your hair has picked up information and projected impressions of you to everyone in your environment. Our efforts to create specific impressions with our hair can involve a great deal of time and money over our lifetime. After our bodies pass on, our hair, holding our DNA and our story, can remain for thousands of years. It is ageless and mysterious like our soul.

We love the concept of 'gardening our hair.' In our holistic approach, which views hair as interconnected with our whole being, we care for hair as we would tend a garden or a cherished plant. Scientific research has produced significant evidence that plants are affected by what we say to them, think about them, and what we do to them. Nurturing plants may involve cutting, watering, fertilizing, talking to, or even playing music for them. Our hair is similar to plants in many ways. First of all, it grows! The healthier it is, the better and more beautifully it grows. And, hair has consciousness! As a living part of our body, our hair is actually affected by and responsive to its environment. Our hair also reacts to what we say about it, think about it, and how we treat it.

Hair is influenced by many biological processes within our bodies. The proper kinds of nutrients including proteins, vitamins, minerals, oils, and water, all dramatically influence the health of the hair. The lack of these creates a negative impact. The fact that we refer to hair as healthy or unhealthy shows that we experience it as a living part of us. Rocks and crystals have energy, but are only affected by geological processes not biological processes like our magical hair.

Noticing how our hair behaves when we are sick, shows very clearly how our body's functions are linked. Our hair can look dull, limp, or oily, not just because we are bedridden and it is too much effort to wash the hair. The body withdraws its energy from the hair to focus on the areas that need the most attention. Lungs, kidneys, bladder, spleen, pancreas, heart, liver, and brain are top priority. Hair is not necessary for survival. Consequently during an illness, hair can hang down like an under-watered plant. Once the body is back in shape, the hair recovers.

We will explore hair from angles and perspectives you may never have considered. The section, *Yin and Yang of Hair Care* suggests many options to help you choose what is right for your hair, and what fits your personal style of hair care. Under the section, *Nature's Elements* you will find our recommendations organized with both inner and outer ways of enhancing the health of your hair. What resonates with you, will become a part of *Your Personal Hair Care Plan*, which you can easily incorporate into your daily life. The sun and moon cycles are directly and existentially connected to our lives, and we will illuminate and explain how they influence our hair. Environmentally conscious hair care is fun, creative, and rewarding. We will show you how to make a difference with just five easy steps.

When hair is cared for with appreciation and knowledge, it opens up to the cosmos as vibrant antenna. Your hair is an incredible force. It can attract potential partners, receive information and awareness, as well as communicate and radiate your intentions. These functions are encouraged with conscious, holistic, hair care.

Nature's Hair

Trees have leaves
And people have hair.
Black sea, white waves,
Flowing lava, golden sunrays.
The whorl on the head of a newborn
Can unfurl like a storm or
gently unfold as a flower blossom.

EVER PRESENT NATURE

In our Western minds nature has become separate from our lives, an entity of its own. We say 'let's go out into nature this weekend' because we want to escape the exhaust fumes, concrete, and neon lights to breathe fresh air, walk winding paths, and light a fire. In truth, nature is never separate from us. It is within us, around us, and it is part of us. This is similar to our relationship with hair.

Although we are physically connected to our hair, we don't always experience it that way. We often ignore its needs or try to control it as if it were an adversary. Besides being one of the creative ways we express ourselves, our hair is the antenna of our body, extending into the larger space around us that is also nature. It has the ability to perceive and project information. When our hair 'stands on end,' it can indicate a sense of awe, be a verification, or a signal for heightened awareness.

Dr. Christiane Northrup describes goose bumps, when the tiny muscles connected to our hair follicles make the hairs stand on end, as "the way something important makes itself known." She says our hair, through these goose bumps connect us to the larger grid of humanity.

Nature is the ultimate resource for what we need to maximize the health and energetic potential of our hair. Nature is structured into different kingdoms: microorganisms, minerals, plants, animals, and humans. Each interfaces with and depends on the other kingdoms. Hair contains treasures from all of them. It grows like a plant, stores minerals like a stone, and is made of protein, like lamb's wool.

Nature offers a huge spectrum of holistic products and practices from pure water to complex plant formulas. Holistic hair care is much more than the best solutions to hair loss, damaged hair, or chemical allergies. It can have a positive impact on many other aspects of our lives.

OUR HAIR - ROOTS AND ANTENNAE

This perspective of relating to hair as a plant, rooted in our scalp, reveals very practical and easy ways to improve its wellbeing. Before we explore these practices, lets investigate the roots of the antenna theories.

Long before working professionally with hair, we learned about the concept of hair functioning as antenna through studying various yoga practices. We were aware that television and radio used antennae, dogs and cats have sensitive whiskers, insects have feelers. We humans have our hair.

Could it be possible that our hair functions as antenna and we don't even know it? Or is this concept simply a metaphor, and hair is nothing more than dead protein hanging off our heads, as scientists in the early 1900's declared?

Millions of people on this planet regard hair as their very own cosmic antenna. The 25 million Sikhs, members of the fifth largest religion, don't cut their hair, which they call *kesh* because they believe God gave it to them for a reason. Removing it would mean dishonoring a gift from God, or questioning the intelligence and purpose of this gift. They accept that God gave humans the longest hair of all beings to provide vitamins to the brain, especially vitamin D. Not removing hair is one of their five vows. To the Sikhs hair is definitely not just a fashionable appendage but is antennae, for communicating with and being connected to higher forces.

Many cultures and tribes see hair as the extension of the body, which connects the visible to the invisible worlds. In the popular futuristic movie *Avatar*, the Navi people are able to connect their hair to the wings and tails of animals, and meld it into the earth, bonding to nature, each other, and the spirit world. For them, hair is a fundamental mode of connection.

Hawaiian people and Native Americans have very respectful relationships with their hair. There is an amazing article that has circulated the internet for many years titled, *Why Indians Keep Their Hair Long*. It tells the story of a psychologist who worked at a VA Medical hospital, mostly with Vietnam veterans. He accessed information on a study pertaining to hair. The Vietnam War special forces had sent undercover experts to American Indian Reservations looking for experienced scouts, men trained to move silently through the forests. They were especially looking for men with outstanding, almost supernatural sensing abilities. These carefully selected men were extensively documented as experts in tracking and survival. Once enlisted, a shocking thing happened. Whatever talents and skills they possessed on the reservation seemed to mysteriously disappear as recruit after recruit failed to perform as expected in the field. Serious casualties and performance failures led the government to conduct expansive testing of these recruits, and this is what was found.

When questioned about their failure to perform, the older recruits replied consistently that when they received their required military haircuts, they could no longer 'sense' the enemy approaching. Their intuition was no longer reliable, they couldn't read subtle signs, or access extrasensory information. So the testing institute recruited more Indian trackers, let them keep their long hair, and tested them in multiple areas. They would pair two men together who had received the same scores on all the tests. They would let one man in the pair keep his hair long, and gave the other man a military haircut. When the two men retook the tests, the man with long hair kept achieving high scores, while the recruit with the short hair failed the tests.

This concept of hair as an antenna no longer seems so far fetched, does it? Have you ever experienced a situation that made your hairs stand on end? Hair is connected to the nervous, circulatory, and hormonal body systems. This is why over time hair can change its texture, sheen, and other qualities. Hair is an extension of the nervous system with sensitivity to temperature changes and even danger. Hair can store and emit energy, information, and substance. It absorbs sunlight, vitamin D, stores trace elements and minerals, and exudes energy into the electromagnetic field. The latter can be demonstrated with Kirlian photography, which captures an image of the energy field around living things.

To consider the possibility that each hair is actually a highly evolved antenna or feeler that transmits information to the brain, let us look at how antennae are constructed and how that compares to hair. Antennae are often coiled,

sometimes in a helix, and so is hair. The structure of our DNA is a double helix. Antennae and hair follow the geometry of the spiral. Hair grows out of the scalp in a spiral. Throughout the ages, yogis have spiraled their hair into a bun on top of the head to concentrate energy at the crown chakra. Does this mean if we want to advance in our meditation practice or be in the CIA, we cannot cut our hair anymore? What about monks or nuns who shave their hair to minimize distraction from their spiritual focus?

When we view hair as an antenna, it might seem that people with short or no hair are disadvantaged. That is not necessarily so. Very short hair and even a bald head can also receive light, store protein and minerals, as well as pick up and send out energy.

Every hair on a bald or shaved head is in a nearly perfect ratio with regard to the cranium therefore being close to 100% in balance. What most influences hairs' function as antenna is the physical health of the hair and the way it is cut.

The healing art of Hair Balancing enhances all functions of hair using a pattern of sacred geometry, which can be applied to any length or style. Hair Balancing is an ultra-precise holistic hair cutting system based on the principles of acupuncture and cranio-sacral therapy. Hair Balancing bevels the hair with the clean, sharp lines you might see on the ends of a crystal. This improves the antenna function, while also creating aerodynamic movement to the hair, allowing it to move freely through space.

Hair Balancing awakens the sense of how hair feels in addition to the visual experience of how it looks. As hairs grow further from their root connection in the scalp, the Hair Balancing cutting process maintains the proper ratio among all the hairs to facilitate energy flow, beauty and balance. Some clients call it Feng Shui for the hair.

What we gain from this concept is the understanding that our hair has the potential to assist us in extrasensory perception, so the healthier it is the better it will function. Consciously caring for our hair from the root out is a necessary first step in enhancing its antenna power.

THE POWER OF HAIR GARDENING

Hair grows like a plant out of the unique soil of the scalp. Seeing hair in the context of nature and applying nature's laws, we become gardeners of hair, who prune and care for our hair like a precious flowering plant or bush. In a garden, the right nutrients must be in the soil, and the proper amount of sun and water, must all be in balance to grow the healthiest plants possible. The same is true for our hair.

Some people dislike their hair, regarding it as the bane of their existence. Sometimes after listening to them describe all the negatives of their hair, we suggest, "At least you have hair." Imagining the contrast of having 'no hair at all' can sometimes elicit a small amount of gratitude for at least having some hair. This can be a starting point for developing a relationship of acceptance that can grow over time into appreciation, eventually flowering into a truly happy relationship.

Talking to your hair,
Watering your hair,
Pruning your hair,   **=**   **Happy Hair**
Stimulating your hair,   **Happy You**
and of course...
Loving your hair.

Your hair wants to please you. It wants to be the hair you love. But if it keeps hearing itself described as "too thick, too thin, too curly, too straight, too frizzy, won't grow, falling out, dry, blah, or split, and broken," it is locked into that description and has no opportunity to evolve into the hair you would prefer to have. Our mind does not always know the difference between what is real and what is imagined. If one expresses gratitude for their hair becoming thicker, having more body, growing faster, or whatever intention is being held for their ultimate hair, all the cells involved in growing hair 'act as if' and support the hair developing those qualities. We agree with Dr. Christiane Northrup who states, "Words matter, they have an impact on your biology. Your beliefs and expectations are far more important than genes or environment."

If the right conditions are put into place miracles can happen. Applying the practices to your hair that you would use to nurture plants is a mindfulness approach that can yield enormously satisfying results.

When your hair is making you happy, that is the time to say, "I love how thick you look," "I love these beautiful waves," or "I love how fast you are growing." Whatever you desire for your hair, start appreciating when your hair is doing something close to that. If your hair is a long way off from your goals, you can still give thanks for what you are intending to manifest. The kinder you are with your hair the more responsive it will be to your desires.

We have actually seen the quality of hair change over time, becoming the hair of one's dreams and imagination. Albert Einstein said, "Imagination is the preview of life's coming attractions." A client who has had her hair balanced for many years, recommends,

> *"When you begin talking with your hair, you might feel it's rather silly or stupid. Don't be disappointed if you can't understand what your hair is saying right away. Take the time to ask your hair what it wants and needs, then listen. It can truly be amazing."*

Hair is with us every moment for most of our lives. Who or what else is with you through it all, the ups and the downs, thick and thin? Think about it. You dance and swim with your hair, go to sleep and wake up with it and care deeply about the image your hair projects to the world.

According to a study directed by Dr. Marianne LaFrance, Professor of Psychology and Professor of Women's and Gender Studies at Yale University, bad hair days affect individuals' self-esteem, increasing self-doubt, intensifying social insecurities, and tends to make them more self-critical in general.

"Interestingly, both women and men are negatively affected by the phenomenon of bad hair days," says Professor LaFrance. The study further found that bad hair intensifies feelings of self-consciousness. The psychological reactions differed among women and men. Women tend to feel more disgraced, embarrassed, ashamed or self-conscious when experiencing bad hair. Men on the other hand, feel more nervous, less confident and are more inclined to be unsociable. "Even more fascinating is the finding that individuals perceive their capabilities to be significantly lower than others when experiencing bad hair." Using guidance from nature you can create great hair days and improve the quality of your life.

In the chapter, Nature's Elements you will find many suggestions of how to water, prune, stimulate, and nourish your hair. Notice how your hair responds over time. Consistency will produce the best outcomes.

What Hair Looks Like and How it Grows

Understanding and visualizing how hair develops and functions is the foundation of creating healthy and vibrant hair.

Each hair consists of the root, located beneath the scalp or skin's surface, embedded within the follicle, and the hair shaft, which is the visible part extending above the surface. The hair follicle is the indentation in your scalp, enclosing the root. Follicles can be different sizes, and there is one follicle for each hair. One or two sebaceous glands, also called oil glands, are located next to the follicle and provide oil, which moisturizes the hair shaft and gives it shine and strength.

The very bottom of the hair root, often called the bulb, wraps around the papilla, which is fed by the blood vessels and is responsible for producing new hair cells.

The hair follicle is attached to the arrector pili muscle, which will contract when the body experiences cold temperatures, emotional shock or a sense of danger.

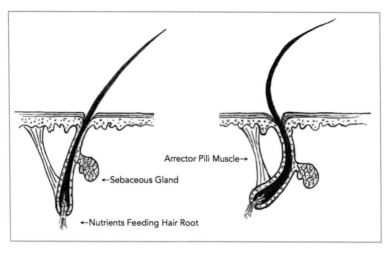

Arrector Pili Muscle→

←Sebaceous Gland

←Nutrients Feeding Hair Root

So even without nerve endings present in the hair shaft, we still can pick up tactile sensations through the root connection. If the follicle lies straight under the scalp, the hair will grow out straight. If it grows beneath the scalp in a curve, the hair will follow that curve and grow in waves or curls.

The texture and shape of some people's hair can change several times throughout their lifetime, while other people have the same type of hair from birth to death. Of course genetic factors play a role, so do hormonal influences and the mysterious interplay of psyche and body.

By definition, a living cell is a cell that reproduces itself. This definition of 'living,' definitely applies to the hair root hidden in the 'soil' of the scalp, but not to the hair shaft. Unfortunately, from this limited perspective, the visual part of the hair has been regarded as dead. This point of view supports the belief that hair can be environmentally or chemically affected without any damaging effects on the body or hair. Holistic hair care does not see it that way. There is a visible and tactile spectrum from vibrant to lifeless hair.

If we want to improve the quality of our hair, we do not see it as dead, because that would mean that it is distinct from our life force and us. Healthy hair, in its wholeness, is a masterpiece of living design. It is constantly growing, shining in the sunlight like ebony, copper, or gold when we feel good, and looks sad when we are in poor health or out of balance.

Cross-sectional cuts show that straight hair is round, wavy hair is oval, and curly hair is a flatter oval.

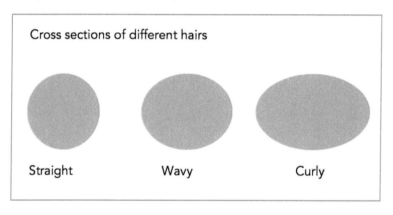

Cross sections of different hairs

Straight   Wavy   Curly

For the alchemists among us, hair consists mainly of the protein keratin. The chemical composition of an average hair is: carbon 50.65%, hydrogen 6.36%, nitrogen 17.14%, sulfur 5.0%, and oxygen 20.85%. This varies with color. Light hair contains less carbon and hydrogen, and more oxygen and sulfur. Dark hair has more carbon and hydrogen, and less oxygen and sulfur.

A hair under the microscope is similar to a tree trunk with its protective bark. It is composed of three different layers. The outer layer is the cuticle, consisting of overlapping horny scales pointing toward the hair end. Try feeling which way they overlap by taking hold of a hair and sliding it between your thumb and forefinger. If you slide toward the root, the hair feels rough because the cuticle is being pushed open against the grain. If you slide toward the end, it feels smooth. The hair is more vulnerable with the cuticle open and more protected with the cuticle closed.

The second layer toward the center is called the cortex, providing elasticity and strength. It also contains the color pigment. The medulla is the third layer, also called the marrow of the hair shaft, which is sometimes missing in very fine hair.

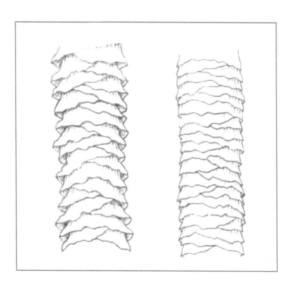

The Growth Cycle of Hair

When a hair falls out, it is usually pushed out of its shaft by a new hair that grows in its place. Sometimes a hair falls out and the potential new hair stays in a dormant state, remaining very fine and short. If we take a section of our head and observe a group of hairs, we will notice that some of them are actively growing, which is called the anagen phase. Some hairs are resting, called the catagen phase, while others are falling out, in their telogen phase.

We have about half a million body hairs which stay much longer in the resting phase than head and beard hair. If body hair had a longer anagen phase, we would look like shaggy bears. Just as our skin renews itself without our noticing it, our body hairs continue to fall out and grow back.

The life span of head hair is usually estimated to be four to eight years. It is commonly accepted that hair grows an average of a half an inch each month or six inches per year. This average comes from a very wide range of hair growth rhythms. There are individuals who can grow nearly an inch a month, and others who observe their hair barely grows. Length is just as variable. Some men and women have grown their hair longer than their actual body length, while others are unable to grow it past their shoulders. One of the most effective ways to achieve greater length is the Hair Balancing cutting method, which facilitates the ability to grow and sustain longer hair even when that was previously a challenge.

Let's get back to some fun hair facts. An average-sized scalp covers about 120 square inches. You'll find an average of 1,000 hairs in one square inch. The number of hairs on the head will vary with the color of the hair. Typically, blond has 140,000, brown has 110,000, black has 108,000, and red has approximately 90,000. Of course there are exceptions to all generalities. Considering how slender each strand is, hair woven together is amazingly strong. When head hair is twisted into a rope, it becomes like aluminum and can hold the weight of a small car!

Many Kinds of Hair on One Body

Our human bodies are covered to various degrees with hair, but not enough to protect us from climate, thorns, teeth and weapons. Unlike animals, we have to look for clothing, materials of a warm or hairy nature, to replace the missing layer. Still, as a biological remainder of fur, the main physical purpose of most hair is protection. Beyond protection, there is even more meaning to the hair in our lives. As a species, we have at least seven types of hair with many different functions. The first is the hair on our heads. This hair may provide some protection against cold weather, wind, or sun, and in some situations can serve as a buffer for head injuries. The Sikh warriors traditionally wove their long hair into their turbans to provide a strong defense against weapons wielded at their heads. If the turban was wrapped outside the hair, it could be knocked off too easily, providing far less protection. Now in other cases, head hair can sometimes make a person more vulnerable. An enemy or aggressor could grab and pull the hair, so some soldiers and warriors choose to wear their hair short, shaved, or covered.

Since ancient times hair has been arranged as an attractive adornment, and has been a vital consideration in mating rituals with the goal of procreation. Head hair in the modern world is mostly about style and self-expression.

Beard hair is usually a gender sign, distinguishing men from women. Beards and all their variations, have gone in and out of vogue for centuries. They can be an expression of virility or a back to nature way of life. Certain ethnic groups genetically have less beard hair than others, and some, like Native Americans or Eskimos, have almost none. Beards and moustaches are often required or sometimes forbidden by different organizations or religious groups. Yet they provide many men, the creative options to adorn, cover, or reveal their faces however they please. These variations may also be used to look more attractive for mating, or fiercer for battle.

Eyebrows and eyelashes serve to protect the eyes and therefore our vision. Eyebrows keep salty sweat away from eyes, while eyelashes protect them from dust particles, also reducing light glare. Both function as adornments and flirtation devices. These have a shorter life span than head and beard hair and are replaced every four to five months.

Nose and ear hairs have an important filtering function as they protect our lungs and ears. They often increase in men as they age, although the benefits are not fully understood or appreciated.

Pubic hair appears at the beginning of puberty, announcing sexual maturity and tends to fade away in the latter stages of life. Pubic hair also serves as a protective cushion. It keeps the genitals from rubbing against clothes. Pubic hair may ease the friction of passionate movement, while it also supports the creation of an electro-magnetic environment designed for conceiving a child. Underarm hair also functions as a buffer, as the skin can become irritated from sweating. It also holds the sweat and pheromones that attract or repel sexual partners.

Men usually have much more body hair than women, creating a secondary gender mark. This is called terminal or androgenic hair. If we look at body hair as a microcosmic equivalent of the Earth's vegetation; body hair is like grass or moss. Hair can be found all over the body's surface except on the palms, soles of our feet, eyelids, and mouth. Vellus hair is how we describe the fine hair on the cheeks, forehead, and many other areas of the body. These hairs assist in the evaporation of perspiration, and they do a great job keeping us from being damp and clammy.

Hair can inform us about the health and age of a person. If hair does not grow or is falling out, it can be the body's warning sign to check the state of the inner organs and systems that we cannot see. It is often the first indication that there are physical, emotional, psychological or even environmental problems. Hair loss is a signal to stop, look, and listen to your hair and body.

Laura and Linda have both experienced significant hair loss on several occasions throughout their lives resulting in compassion for anyone suffering from hair loss and the acquisition of many tools to remedy the condition.

Your Hair's Special Gift

Answering the following questions will deepen the relationship with your hair.

What are your strongest memories relating to your hair?

What role does your hair play in your life right now?

What has your hair taught you?

How is it connected to your dreams and visions?

If you had to choose one, what is your hair's special gift to you?

THE YIN AND YANG OF HAIR CARE

The Yin Yang symbol represents wholeness, the total balance of opposites, especially of the feminine and masculine and light and dark aspects in this world. It can be a way of viewing any area of life. The two dots in the center of each side of the symbol portray the fact that within the Yin there is the Yang element and vice versa. For everything in life, its opposite also exists; summer and winter, hot and cold, mean and kind, up and down, in and out.

The chart to the right gives you an idea, how the principle of Yin and Yang can be helpful with regard to hair care. When you read the two lists, note what might be beneficial right now for your hair, more Yin or Yang, or a little bit of both.

Yin	Yang
Feeling what your hair needs	Deciding what to do with your hair
Feeling when it's time for a haircut	Taking action, making an appointment
A female/feminine hairdresser	A male/masculine hairdresser
Caressing and nurturing	Initiating change
Support from the inside	Support from the outside
Nutrition, mental attitude	Holistic products and conscious hair practices
Taking care of the hair you have	Cutting off what you don't want
Intuitive reasons for getting a haircut	Practical reasons for getting a haircut
Moonlight	Sunlight
Comb/combing	Scissors/cutting
Root	Antenna

Although in most depictions of yin and yang symbology the two sides appear very distinct from one another, in real life there is an infinite spectrum between all polarities, blurring some distinctions between the two. These heart-shaped stones tend to be light toward one side and dark toward the other. The lines between each polarity are blurred in both stones. Each is unique, while also being quite similar. This reminds us of the nuances of most situations, including how we care for our hair. Wouldn't it be nice if there was simply one right way that was appropriate for all of us? As most of us have discovered, that is not the case. We are all such uniquely different bio-chemical organisms that we must determine the best products and practices for each of us to achieve the optimal results for our hair. This involves knowing your specific hair type, which many people are surprisingly confused about, and will help you understand how certain products and ingredients might work with your hair. Like many things in life, this can be a process of trial and error.

WHAT KIND OF HAIR DO YOU HAVE?

Many people have mistaken notions about what the quality and texture of their hair actually is. Often this is due to a comment that was made to them by a friend, parent, or hairdresser, which imprinted some unconscious limitations regarding their hair. Most people do not have the opportunity to touch, comb, brush or play with many other people's hair. Therefore they have a limited perspective of what other types of hair feel like, giving them very little basis for comparison. There is also a societal pressure toward modesty, which makes it difficult to genuinely accept a compliment or the simple fact that you might have lovely hair. We are trained to look for fault in our appearance and point it out so we won't appear too self-centered.

Often clients will describe their hair as thin or fine, when it is actually medium or average with regard to thickness and density. Some have experienced occasions when a hairdresser, unable to create the result their client was looking for, blames the hair; describing it as too fine, too coarse, too thick, too thin, too straight, or too curly. This serves to shield them from responsibility as the stylist, while leaving the client believing they have 'bad' or 'difficult' hair. Unfortunately these negative descriptions can stay embedded in a person's mind and psyche, often for the rest of their life.

Each marvelous hair on your head, can be defined by its length, width, density, and pattern. These characteristics will help you determine the specific care your hair needs.

This is about empowering you, the owner of your hair, to forge a whole new relationship with your hair, based on understanding what it is and what it needs.

Length

First, we categorize the length of hair as either very short/bald, short; which is not longer than chin length, medium length; usually mid-neck and no longer than shoulders, and long hair; which is past the shoulders.

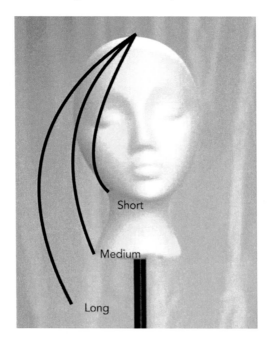

Width

Next, the width of your individual hairs determines whether your hair is described as ultra-fine, fine, medium, thick, or extra thick, sometimes called coarse. Commonly people refer to width by saying how thick their hair is. As long as the thickness spectrum is referring to the width of the individual hair shafts, it is clear. Confusion is created when people also describe the amount of hair on their heads as thick or thin. That quality we describe as density.

There is a spectrum of widths. The majority of us fall somewhere in between. It might help to think of the various thicknesses of hair like thread or yarn, which comes in a variety of widths. The width of normal sewing thread is equal to 8-10 hairs. Most newborn babies have very fine hair, which usually becomes thicker and changes throughout their lifetime. There are some people who retain that ultrafine texture throughout their lives and find it almost impossible to style or control. Many resort to permanent waves to make it submit. If your hair is not that baby fine wisp of hair, you may still have fine hair, but there are definitely degrees of fineness. The finer the hair the more fragile it is. Exceptionally coarse hair, often referred to as horsehair, is very strong and resilient. It can usually withstand environmental stress and chemical processing much better than normal to fine hair.

Density

Density describes the amount of hairs you have on your head and how close they are to one another. Think of it as the number of hairs per square inch. Density is also referred to as hair volume, described as low, medium, or high. The appearance of volume is often created with products, which is another reason the word density is a more accurate description. Imagine the dots below as individual hairs.

High Density   Medium Density   Low Density

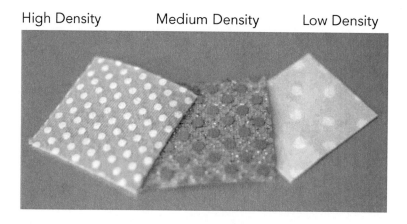

Hair of
average
density

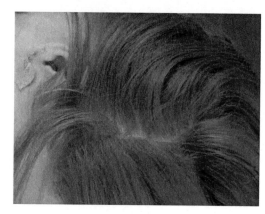

Pattern

The pattern, also known as texture of your hair, is most often expressed as straight, wavy, curly, or tightly coiled. These descriptive words are mostly self-explanatory, although the qualities they describe are not fixed realities. Some people find the patterns of their hair can change over time and even be quite different from one part of the head to another at the same time. Age, health, genetics, hair cutting techniques, environment, hormones, chemotherapy and simply training the hair, can change the pattern. And it has been known to change with no apparent reason. Hair still holds many mysteries.

Straight, as well as wavy and curly hair can be fine or normal or coarse. People erroneously assume that African American hair is coarse, when usually it is quite fine and subject to breaking easily.

Some ethnicities, such as Sicilians have a lot of high density, thick (maximum width), wavy hair. Asian hair is predominantly straight and tends to be thicker and more coarse than most Caucasian hair. Scandinavian hair is also predominantly straight, yet finer in width. These are broad generalities, and with the genetic tumbler of the world today, new varieties of hair are created every moment.

Here you can see these four examples of the actual same length looking very different because of the curling pattern. That's why it takes curly hair more time to appear long.

Natural volume derives from the density of the hair, which is equivalent to the amount of hair on the head, not necessarily the thickness of the individual hairs. A person can have a dense head full of very fine hairs.

Or one could have a very sparse amount of hair on the head, which could be comprised of wiry, coarse hairs. In conversations about hair, we want to be clear about the volume; referring to the density of hair on the head, versus the width of the individual hairs.

A quality of your hair that can change radically over time, is oiliness or dryness. This directly influences how often one washes and what products and style choices are best. Most people with oily hair employ various tactics to minimize the visible effects of the excess oil. Surprisingly, washing less frequently can help your scalp to not over-produce oil. Using dry shampoos made of organic cornstarch can also be helpful in absorbing excess oil.

The person with dry hair often misjudges the degree of dryness even believing it to be split or broken. When examined closely, we discover that often it is not that damaged. Hair can be so dry that it will not lay right or form a wave or curl properly. Just as with a plant, that damage needs to be trimmed off to allow the life force to focus on new growth, rather than being wasted trying to regenerate damaged hair. Removing the dry ends liberates the healthy hair to a gorgeous new experience of itself.

Know your hair, know thyself!

Circle or mark the characteristics of your hair.

Pattern	Straight	Wavy	Curly	Coiled
Length	Very Short	Short	Medium	Long
Width	Very Fine	Fine	Medium	Thick/Coarse
Density	Sparse	Low	Medium	High

DISCOVER YOUR HAIR CARE STYLE

Our hair clients have taught us that everyone has different priorities and needs when it comes to hair care. Even among Hair Balancing practitioners we find we can be quite different. When it comes to hair care and styling routine, Linda is the quintessential minimalist. She uses one product for her scalp and body, and one brush. That's it. No styling products or tools, except a blow dryer in the winter when it is really cold outside and a moisturizing spray when it is very dry.

After Hair Balancing brought out the natural curl in Laura's formerly straight hair, she continues to experiment with several different products to achieve the quality of curl she desires. And over the years as her hair has become more dry, she continues trying different oils and other products to address dryness and frizz which seems to increase with the number of gray hairs. These make her hair care style mostly 'curious' as she is always researching and investigating new healthy products. Basically she washes with moisturizing shampoos, uses both a rinse out and a leave-in conditioner, and lets her hair air dry naturally, which is the simplicity of wash and wear.

Finding out what is most important to you, helps refine your hair care routine to what is most comfortable for you. It will allow you to reduce judgments towards yourself and those around you. There is not one right way. What one person needs or wants to do with their hair will be completely different for someone else. Read the following descriptions to see what styles you find yourself resonating with. Have fun selecting your dominant hair care style. You may find you choose elements from different styles. These may also change over time. The woman who loved pampering herself, may find she becomes a minimalist when coping with her newborn. An absolute constant in life is change, and within all that change, you are still you, but your hair may change over time.

Pampering

Do you love to play with and pamper yourself with many different products and habits? Do you use this time to connect with yourself and to relax? Do various scents and treatments enrich the quality of your life? Some clients who enjoy pampering discover they have been attracted to products containing harmful chemicals and artificial fragrances. When they explore and experiment with sensually pleasurable and life-enhancing, healthy alternatives, they never look back.

Yes, that's me!	Sometimes I like to pamper myself.	I don't spend much time pampering myself.

Minimalist

Do you like an efficient routine, which saves you time, energy and money? Are you very happy with one product, which you use for years? Are you not really interested in trying something new, since what you have works well?

Yes, that's me!	In some areas of my life I like to be minimalistic.	The variety life offers is hard to pass by.

Concerned

Is health your top priority? Are you concerned about the health of your scalp and hair? Do you take vitamins and minerals, as well as exercise and eat well? Do you want to learn as much as possible about health and how to improve it? Are you driven to find the best solutions for you and your hair? Those with a Concerned hair care style might avoid products from companies which test on animals, or make sure that all ingredients in their products are organic, naturally sourced, or wild-crafted.

Yes, that's me!	Health is important but I try not to be rigid.	Life is too short to worry too much.

Curious

Do you like to experiment and try many different products and techniques? Do you enjoy variety? Does your hair seem to perform better when you mix and match with different products?

Yes, that's me!	I like to explore, always checking out new products.	I find all the choices overwhelming.

NATURE'S ELEMENTS FOR YOUR HAIR

Nature consists of earth, bodies of water, sun and moonlight, winds, gases, and energy. Nature takes care of itself with the power of the five elements Earth, Water, Fire, Air, and Ether constantly striving for balance among them.

We are made of the same five elements: bones and flesh of the Earth, water, lymph and blood from the Water element, muscles expressing Fire, breath is of the Air, and life energy expresses Ether. Our hair and nails, which last much longer after death than other body parts, have common constituents with flesh and bone, and are considered part of the earth element.

The hair root is a little factory using mineral nutrients from the blood and water, to create new hair. The sebaceous glands produce the necessary oil. Hair transmits energy and is electrically charged, representing the fire element. We are merging the qualities of ether with the air element, because ether's ethereal quality is more difficult to see and quantify. Breath, our life force reaches beyond our bodies, all the way through and beyond the tips of our hair.

These four elements complement and balance each other as combinations of the hot to cold and the dry to moist spectrums. Earth is hot and moist. Water is cold and moist. Fire is hot and dry. Air is cold and dry.

To achieve healthy hair, we need to determine if it is lacking or has too much of a specific element. For example, if your hair exhibits signs of too much air, the realm of cold to dry, you can balance the air with earth's hot to moist qualities, which is the domain of invigorating and soothing plant-based products. A clear henna conditioning treatment, an avocado pack or various oils may restore the balance. Understanding these aspects of nature's elements helps us bring them into their proper balance.

Hair grows from the inside out. If we want to improve the condition of our hair, we have to approach it from the inside as well as the outside. For example, for dry hair, we can externally apply moisturizing products and oils, and from the inside we can eat high quality foods and drink more life-enhancing water.

Now you can begin designing your personal Hair Care Improvement Plan. You will see that each of the following elements is grouped into one Inside and several Outside aspects. While reading through them, note what you are already doing, and what might be changed or incorporated to improve your hair care results. Mark what you are already doing with a check √ right next to the topic and use an exclamation mark ! for areas that could use improvement or be replaced with new practices. When you read through all four elements, transfer the checks and exclamation marks onto the overview at the end of this chapter.

Earth – Nurturing – Yin

Eating Well for Your Hair

The Earth element forms the basis of hair care and provides us with plant extracts, clays, and minerals, materials for combs and brushes, as well as our food. Healthy hair requires protein, and a full spectrum of vitamins, and minerals, especially the trace minerals. These are small amounts of extremely essential minerals that are found most abundantly in the Himalayas, salty inland seas, and special coastal areas, such as Brittany, France. Eating for healthy hair may require additional

FROM THE INSIDE

supplementation, as it is often difficult to receive enough minerals from our diet. Hair and skin both require rich oils like olive, coconut, sesame, and flax. The quality is very important; look for organic, cold-pressed oils and be sure to include oils that are high in Omega-3 fatty acids. When we eat for the well being of our hair, we nourish the hair from the inside.

It is important to note that for some people certain foods can precipitate unwanted scalp conditions and hair loss. Gluten intolerance has been linked to alopecia, which causes hair loss in certain areas. Food allergies can also trigger inflammation of the scalp, which is also associated with hair loss. Hair loss is such a vast topic with so many different aspects that it is the subject of our next book.

Food for Your Hair

Next time when you go food shopping let your hair take the lead. Allow your body and hair to be attracted to and respond viscerally and visually to the foods that would be beneficial for you.

The Right Shampoo

What we put on our hair and scalp hopefully is nourishing it from the outside. Anything we absorb through the pores of our body has both a direct and an indirect effect on our hair. One of the most commonly used hair products is shampoo. Some people are fine with using any shampoo, believing soap is soap. Others make more refined choices about the ingredients for nourishing their hair, which will be absorbed by the capillaries in their scalp into their blood stream. Harmful ingredients could be deposited in the brain, skin, eyes, or inner ear as the blood carries them along.

FROM THE OUTSIDE

You need two things when shopping for shampoos: your eyes and your nose. Your eyes are there to read the back label with the ingredient list, not just the keywords on the front of the bottle. You are checking for unwanted, unnecessary chemicals and looking for the best ingredients for your hair type.

When you find too many ingredients listed that you don't understand, these are likely to be drying alcohols, preservatives, foaming agents, artificial colors, fragrances, and other additives that could irritate, coat, and dry out your scalp and hair. Shampoo manufacturers do not have to list all ingredients and can avoid being specific.

To make things easier for you, at the end of this book you will find a list of the ingredients you most want to avoid in your personal care products. You definitely want

to avoid surfactants like sodium lauryl sulfate and most other sulfates which clean the hair too well. These sudsing agents are found in laundry detergents, dishwashing liquids, and engine degreasers. They strip off the hair's natural protective oils. Our bodies store sodium lauryl sulfate and related chemicals which can cause or contribute to chemical sensitivities, dermatitis and allergies. Most sulfates are produced synthetically, but on many labels, are listed as derived from coconut. This creates the impression of being a natural product when in fact, it is still a drying synthetic formula far removed from the coconut source. Lauryl sulfate was developed in 1952 in the United States to aid in the removal of motor oils from engines. Since then it has hidden under at least twenty different names in our shampoos, face and body washes, toothpastes, and other personal care products.

Shopping at a health food store or choosing environmentally conscious packaging of hair care products is no guarantee of purity. At least 90% of all shampoos currently on the market contain chemical ingredients. Sometimes a few herbal or even organic ingredients are added and promoted on the front of the bottle, creating the illusion that a shampoo is good for you, when it may not be the case at all.

The most misleading word on product labels is 'natural.' It does not mean organic or free of GMOs. Always ignore the word 'natural' and read the ingredient label for accurate information. Choose products from companies that you trust as you learn to decode labels. If you are not familiar with the standards of the manufacturers, ask the person working in that department of your local health food store for information and recommendations.

Shampoos that promise to clean the follicles thoroughly appeal to our goal of cleanliness to an extreme. We want products and a routine that will bring our hair into a healthier, balanced state. Some products claim to unplug hair follicles, so consumers will believe that their hair won't grow because it is suffocating under a buildup of bacteria, germs, and sebum. What actually happens more frequently is that the chemicals in shampoos and styling aids can build up and weaken the scalp's immunity providing a breeding ground for bacteria. The chemicals throw the sebaceous glands out of balance, which react by either over- or under-producing sebum. Using chemicals to 'unplug' them can create a vicious circle of cleaning the follicles while we continue to damage the scalp's natural pH balance and immunity.

There is one solution: nourish the sensitive eco-system in which your hair grows with 100% truly natural ingredients. They will support your body's self-cleaning and self-regulating abilities.

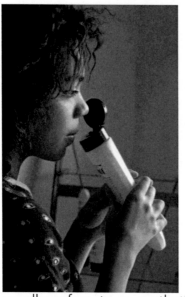

Once you are satisfied with the ingredient list, it is time to open the cap and sniff. Your nose tells you immediately whether you like the product, and whether it is right for you personally. The fragrance of a substance should invite you to use it, or could be a strong indicator that it is not right for you. The word fragrance on the label usually refers to a synthetic, solvent-based smell. We prefer essential oils or no fragrance added at all, just the pure plant and mineral ingredients.

When you switch from mainstream commercial to healthier products, it can be advantageous to rotate between at least two natural shampoos keeping the scalp's immune system stimulated and strong. Rotating shampoos has been helpful for itchy, irritated, or scaly scalps. Usually a pure formula with no fragrance or color added is best. Some people like to keep it simple, others enjoy variety. When you wash your hair, observe, which way you and your hair find most beneficial. You may find yourself alternating in a seemingly random way. The body has its inner wisdom, and this is a fun opportunity to work with your intuition, and then assess the results. Your hair and scalp will give you feedback.

Organic Apple Cider Vinegar

Organic unpasteurized apple cider vinegar can be applied directly, usually diluted, onto the scalp in addition to, or instead of, shampooing. It can naturally clean and refresh the pores, restoring the pH balance, and its live enzymes have a delightfully stimulating effect. Sometimes, simply using organic, unpasteurized apple cider vinegar instead of shampoo can ease hair loss and problems like dandruff or itchy scalp. It can also be used as a rinse after shampooing.

Oil Treatments

Raw oil treatments can be applied to moisturize and balance hair and scalp. They can be very effective for taming frizz. Oils are extracted from seeds, nuts, herbs, vegetables, and some fruits. When choosing an oil, consider your hair quality, ethnic background, and current living environment. People from India and Polynesia have been using coconut and sesame oils for their skin and hair for centuries. Some Caucasian hair seems to absorb virgin olive oil or grape seed oil the best. In the Southwest and Mexico, jojoba oil, which is the most similar to our natural secretion of sebum, is a great choice for fairly thick hair. Europeans often use sunflower and wheat germ oils. For the best results, oils should be slightly warmed, applied to dry hair, and left on for at least twenty minutes.

Oils, and also the apple cider vinegar scalp treatment, can be left on all night, just protect your pillow with a towel and if you like you can use a shower or night cap. If you do this in the daytime, sitting in the sun will help it absorb even better.

How to Get an Oil Treatment out of Your Hair

Create lather with the shampoo in your hands and apply it directly on your hair before wetting the hair. Water and oil do not mix, so if you wet your hair first and then add shampoo, you may have to repeat the washing cycle four or five times. By then, you may have stripped off more oil than what you started with, making the benefit of your oil treatment marginal. By applying the lather directly to the oily hair first, you may find one or two washes will remove the excess oil, leaving your hair shiny and soft.

Instead of a full oil treatment, you can always put one or two drops of oil into your hands and then wipe your hands over the outer layers down over the tips of your hair. Argan, grape seed, apricot, or other light oils work well for a little sheen and protection. This way, the hair will absorb a little bit of protective oil without looking greasy. Dry and colder climates with indoor heat can suck moisture from the outer layers and ends of your hair. In fact the indoor winter heat can be far more damaging than summer sun. Applying the oil topically on dry or slightly damp hair, creates a barrier between the moisture we want to keep in our hair and the air that seeks to dehydrate us. That is why it can be especially important to apply some oil after washing or wetting your hair. Some hair will benefit from a small amount of oil applied several times a week or even daily.

Flower Power in Your Hair

Wearing flowers is a timeless and uplifting adornment. Pure plant extracts in the form of herbal teas or aromatherapy oils can enhance the health of our scalp and hair. When the essence of the plant is absorbed, it nurtures the inside and shines around our head like a halo.

Aromatherapy oils are derived from flowers, trees, bushes, seeds, and herbs. These etheric oils are separated from the other parts of the plant through distillation and are highly concentrated. There is a shortage of pure essential oils on the world market, which creates the situation where essential oils are produced to varying standards and many are sold 'cut' or 'engineered.' Research the quality of your sources. We suggest reading the reviews of specific oil suppliers before purchasing.

Aromatherapy oils can be added to massage oils, shampoos and conditioners for therapeutic purposes or to create a pleasing fragrance. Be sure to dilute them with a carrier oil to apply directly on the skin or hair. You can use drops in baths or as perfume, or use in spray bottles and diffusers. You can also put a drop or two on your brush spreading the essential oil into your scalp and hair. Use of essential oils is a highly developed science, having many medicinal and therapeutic applications in addition to elevating mood or energy. We recommend learning more about essential oils for your general health and well-being, but for this book we will only touch on a few oils that are especially beneficial for certain hair types or conditions.

Pure essential oils carry nutrients and oxygen to the cells and are able to pass through the cell walls. When we breathe pure essential oils, the endorphin production and neurotransmitters in our brain register an immediate measurable, positive influence and oxygenation of the body is increased. For hair that is too oily or even greasy with dandruff, try using rosemary, basil, lemon, sage, cypress, cedar wood, or juniper oils. The last three can be combined in equal parts and diluted with a carrier oil. Three to five drops of up to three essential oils mixed in two tablespoons of your carrier oil is a good dilution ratio. You can apply the diluted oil to your scalp, massaging it in and leave for twenty minutes or overnight. Lemongrass is known to slow oil production in the scalp. Frankincense and tea tree oils are anti-fungal and anti-bacterial. They treat and protect hair and scalp from many unwanted conditions like eczema and psoriasis. Occasionally these oils may be too strong and can be irritating. Oil of chamomile can soothe inflammation and help heal scaly scalps.

For dry hair some of the best oils would be rose, lavender, geranium, myrrh, or sandalwood. Cedarwood can balance out a dry scalp as well as an oily one. It will also stimulate hair follicles and is recommended for treating hair loss. Excellent essential oils for normal, healthy hair and scalp are lavender, rosemary, rosewood, frankincense, geranium, clary sage, and chamomile.

Brushing

Daily brushing and scalp massage are time-honored hair care practices, that are often neglected. They increase blood circulation, transport oxygen and precious nutrients to the hair root, and have invigorating and calming effects. Brushing produces the simultaneous effect of dry shampooing and conditioning. It cleans the scalp of buildup, enabling it to breathe freely and secrete its very own precious oils for protecting the hair.

Most brushes with metal and plastic bristles are not able to transport natural hair oils and sometimes irritate scalp and hair. They can also create static electricity. It is best not to share your brush with friends or family. Our unique scalp oil is not as effective when mixed with that of another person. The most beneficial brushing consists of three rounds.

1. The first round is a careful detangling beginning at the ends. Gently use your fingers, a brush, a pick or wide-tooth comb, following the growth direction to avoid combing against the cuticle layer, which could rough it up making it more prone to tangling. Gradually work your way upward.

When the hair is tangle-free, begin brushing the hair from the roots down to the tips, spreading your personal oil over the length of each hair shaft strengthening and protecting them.

2. The next round consists of brush strokes done in the Yin position. Stand or sit with your knees slightly bent and lean forward, directing the flow of blood to the scalp. Start at the nape of the neck, and gently continue over the scalp to the ends of the hair. Brush from around each ear to the ends of the hair in a tender, but firm motion while your hair hangs down. This stimulates the sebaceous glands to produce oil, which is then spread throughout the hair. Instead of hacking into your hair, glide the brush into the hair by tilting the brush at an angle. The brush should touch the skin before moving into the hairline.

Try experimenting with using your non-dominant hand to brush your hair, especially over the opposite side of your head. See how this feels on your neck and shoulders. It may feel awkward at first, but persevere, and you will be amazed how good and balanced it feels over time.

3. The last round of strokes is done in the Yang position. Stand or sit upright and brush the hair back, again starting just before the hairline and spreading the sebum all the way to the tips of the hair by firmly pressing your brush close to the scalp. Try to do as many strokes in the Yang position as in the Yin position. This practice is not intended to style your hair, so right after brushing, you may want to shake your hair and leave it as is, tie it up, or style it the way you like. Your hair may seem oilier immediately after brushing, but the oil should be quickly absorbed by your hair and is desirable for shine.

Most hair benefits from brushing. If, in the beginning you struggle getting the brush through the hair, be patient for at least two weeks. You may need to experiment with different styles of brushes. A boar bristle brush works well for most hair. Very thick and curly hair, often needs a nylon support among the boar bristles. Brushing can straighten curls or even frizz curly hair, but, spritzing with water or diluted aloe vera gel after brushing, often regenerates the curl formation. If hair does not respond enough to spritzing, you may choose to brush only the night before or just prior to washing. The brushing will protect the hair with oil from the scalp so that shampooing will not be as drying. If you do not want to brush your hair, you can stimulate your scalp through either wide tooth combing or scalp massages. If you are experiencing hair thinning, continue brushing gently even if it seems to be pulling out hair. The stimulation and massage is much needed and any hairs that do come out would have fallen out anyway.

Brushing increases your circulation in three important ways. First, the oxygen-rich blood is assisted in flowing into your head feeding your hair follicles, brain, eyes, ears, and skin. Secondly, brushing moves your lymph, which is your internal cleansing fluid flowing throughout the tissues in your body. Lymph moves only when you do. It clears waste and debris from your hair follicles as it cleanses all the functions residing in your head. Bending down or any degree of inversion will enhance this effect. Finally, brushing ushers the energy from the meridians throughout your body into each acupuncture point on the scalp and out beyond the hair, releasing tension and stress.

From a purely physical perspective, brushing clears dust and debris that settles on or in your hair. One of our clients, who always wears her hair up or under a hat finds an extraordinary amount of dust in her brush after her nightly brushing. We are just not aware of how much is in the air that ends up in our hair.

Brush as often as you want, but for straight to gently wavy hair, one to three times a day for two to five minutes is excellent. Brushing with the intention of stimulating hair growth and strengthening the hair, has the most powerful benefit when done before going to sleep.

Brushing is an act of love and nurturing, and we can all use more of that.

Nighttime Brushing

Brushing one's hair before bed is a most sensuous and magnificent way to end your day. It will clear your auric field of the energy and emotions accumulated throughout the day, and release built up stress and strain held in the scalp muscles. It is also a great way to relax your neck and shoulders, where many of us carry so much tension. It is like pressing a reset button. When you first begin brushing, you might feel a bit more invigorated, but if you are tired it will quickly turn into relaxation.

At night, the body's parasympathetic functions are active. The body is not busy running around, eating, and digesting. Instead, it rests, rejuvenates and re-balances itself. When the body is in a horizontal position, blood circulation does not have to push against gravity. It flows with less effort into the head, bathing brain, scalp, hair, and complexion with nutrients and new energy. Night brushing will improve your sleep and enhance your dreams.

Combing

Combing can also be relaxing and invigorating. It may seem to have less impact due to covering less scalp surface per stroke, but the results can be just as soothing as brushing. We find wooden and hard rubber combs are best. When you purchase wooden combs steer clear of those that may develop splinters. Hold them against the light or use a magnifying glass. Once you have found a good wooden comb, it must be oiled from time to time; olive oil works very well. Hard rubber combs are also anti-static. Yet, they do not transport hair oils like wooden combs. Experiment with different widths for the teeth of your combs. A comb with very wide teeth is the best for detangling wet hair. Wet hair should NEVER be brushed. It stretches like elastic when brushed but does not spring back when dry. Over time the hair will loose its elasticity. Combing the hair with a Gemcomb, a comb carved out of a single piece of gemstone, is a harmonizing experience, which benefits the hair, the body, its chakras, and aura.

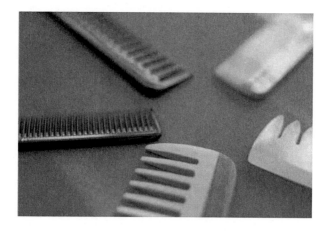

Massaging the Scalp

Massaging the scalp has similar positive effects on blood circulation and sebum production as brushing, while reaching even deeper tissue. It is an excellent technique for those struggling with hair loss to keep the scalp muscles soft and pliable, or for those who choose not to brush. Place fingertips on the scalp with gentle pressure moving the scalp back and forth and from side to side keeping the fingertips in that position. Then place fingertips in another spot and do the same movements. Never rub the fingertips over the surface of the scalp, as it can irritate or loosen hair roots.

Intuitive Pressure

There are numerous acupressure points on the scalp. Let your intuition guide you, with a simple finger pressure technique. Stay with 'press and release' or 'press, wiggle and release' wherever you are guided to go, and you will be fine. This technique can also relieve headaches. You may find yourself experiencing pleasure and relaxation. Massage and press with one or more fingers on tender spots for up to a minute. Let go and feel the tension subside.

Neck and shoulder massages relax neck tension, which allows blood and oxygen to flow more freely into the head. Ideally, the shoulders, neck, and scalp should be loosened up before a haircut, so that the head is more relaxed and energetically connected to the rest of the body.

Scalp Scrubbing

This technique uses a round massage tool made of hard rubber called a scalp scrubber. Firmly but gently massage from the nape of the neck upwards to the forehead. Proceed with a gentle back-and-forth or rotating motion over the entire scalp. This can be done in the shower, before or during shampooing, or while watching television.

Pulling the Hair with a Fist

Grab a small section of hair close to the roots and pull in a direction perpendicular to the scalp. Think of your head as the sun, and each hair is a ray emanating from that sun. Pull at the angle the ray would extend from the sun. This angle will change at every position on the head. It is important not to pull the hair from a non-perpendicular angle, or it will feel uncomfortable and can create stress in the scalp muscles. Don't worry about tearing hair out. If hair is pulled straight, at a precise 90 degree angle, it is incredibly strong and stays connected to the scalp. This Shiatsu massage technique strengthens roots and muscle fibers and can be quite pleasurable.

Water – Refreshing – Yin

Drinking Water for your Hair

Drinking and bathing water, rain, ocean, swimming pool, and hot tub water all affect our hair. The water we drink, cook with, and shower in can be contaminated with heavy metals and chlorine, contributing to dry, weak, and brittle hair. A water filtration system is essential for our internal water consumption, and is very beneficial for bathing and washing hair. Drinking enough pure living water is very important for the health of our scalp and hair. As babies and children we are 75% water. By the time we are 50, we are only 50% water. We dehydrate as we age,

FROM THE INSIDE

creating thinner and less resilient skin and hair. When the body shows signs of dryness, it usually means the body needs more water from the inside. When we feel thirsty, it is usually past the time we need to replenish our inner waters. Drinking a huge bottle or glass of water at once does not rehydrate as one might imagine. Our bodies can only absorb about four ounces at a time, so it is best to spread out water consumption over the day and evening. Otherwise we end up eliminating more than hydrating.

An Ayurvedic doctor shared with us that adding chia seeds to our drinking water helps hydrate the body. Chia seeds absorb the water, swell, and then release the water within the body slowly. Try one teaspoon per glass and see if you seem better able to hold the water in your system instead of eliminating it quickly.

FROM THE OUTSIDE

The Purifying Effect of Water

Oxygen-rich, living water is itself an amazing cleanser. Sometimes it is important to simply rinse your hair just to wash off an intense or unpleasant experience. The Water element is ruled by the moon and stands for our emotional side. If you are emotionally stuck, angry or sad, wash your hair and see what it does for you. It can change or restore your energy right away.

Water Filtration, Showers, and Bottled Water

In an unfiltered ten minute shower, we absorb more chlorine through our skin and lungs than we would from drinking a quart of chlorinated water. We highly recommend a filter attached to your showerhead. If your hair feels dry or sticky after a shower, or especially if you can smell chlorine, a good filter can dramatically change your bathing experience. Hair will become more silky and manageable, and skin will be softer as well.

Water quality can have unpredictable and often undesirable effects on your hair. The hardness of water plays a major role in how your hair looks and feels. For example, we have had clients living in expensive homes in Malibu, who are unable to wash their hair at home. Their well water is so hard and highly mineralized that it damages, even breaks the hair. The same is true for some wonderful mineral hot springs you may enjoy bathing in. They can have great healing powers for your skin but you may want to consider oiling your hair before going into the water to repel the minerals, or even better, put your hair up so the water doesn't touch it.

We have seen the combination of natural personal care products and hard water cause buildup on the hair. In this case, washing and rinsing the hair repeatedly with bottled purified water can clear the buildup. The luxury of rinsing your hair with bottled water is not just for models and actors but for all travelers wanting a consistent water quality.

Many clients who have started to use natural products for their hair, like simple soaps or homemade recipes, have come to us thinking that buildup in their hair is an effect of detoxification from either their previous diets or hair care routines. Buildup on the hair is rarely a sign of detoxification, but is usually a mixture of hair oils, natural product residue, and hard water. Most natural clays and very simple shampooing recipes only work well with soft water.

When the scalp is detoxifying it demonstrates it through dandruff, smells, and excess oils being expelled. None of these create a film-like buildup. Excess oils will make the scalp feel oily, not sticky or coated.

Washing Your Hair with Bottled Water

Use a bottle containing the following amount of water for short to medium hair:
1.5 liters = 6 cups = 1.5 quarts = 50 ounces
Take one third of the water and heat it up, then mix it with another third of the water to achieve a temperature of warm but not hot water. Then take a teaspoon to a tablespoon of shampoo into the palm of your hand mix it with a little bit of bottled water and then apply directly onto the scalp.
Spread the shampoo with a massaging motion over the scalp's surface. Then take the warm water and rinse out. Use the last third of the cool or room temperature water for a final rinse.

Waters

Water bodies like the ocean, lakes, or waterfalls can source rich and vital nutrients for the scalp and hair. It is wonderfully refreshing to massage the scalp under ocean or river water. The scalp will easily absorb the chi, the inherent life energy, as well as the minerals. Sea salt water can help with scalp disorders such as dandruff, itchy scalp, or even hair loss. Sea salt can be added to your clean water to treat scalp conditions, especially dandruff. As beneficial as this can be, you will still want to rinse salt water from your hair, or the salt can become itchy or drying.

Other Waters

Swimming pools and hot tubs usually contain chlorine, ph adjustors, and cleaning detergents. To avoid soaking up all these chemicals, if you cannot keep your hair out of the water, at least wet your hair first, with tap water or filtered water, before jumping into the pool so the hair will not absorb so much of the chlorinated water. You could coat your hair with oil and put it in braids to repel the chlorinated water, or apply conditioner to the hair, then put on a swim cap to prevent hair from absorbing the chlorine. After the swim, rinse conditioner from the hair and you are ready to go, no shampoo needed! Always thoroughly rinse or shampoo your hair after exposure to heavy chlorine. Following up with some type of conditioner or oil to help restore the natural texture.

Water filtration technology is also available for swimming pools and spas. More people are filling their pools and spas with 'living,' oxygen-rich water that is chlorine-free and seeking out the healthiest ways to keep the water clean.

How to Shampoo

Attention! Do not use hot water on your head! Heat expands the pores on your scalp and can cause unwanted hair loss. You can have the water as hot as you like on your body from the neck on down, but be sure to turn it down to lukewarm for wetting and rinsing your hair.

Take enough time with shampooing, cover the whole scalp, especially the back at the nape of the neck, and rinse thoroughly. The scalp has some of the largest pores of the body and absorbs anything it is exposed to within two minutes. If you are using a shampoo with nourishing or therapeutic ingredients, you want to make sure it has time to penetrate the skin. Two minutes can be longer than you think. Time yourself until you get a feel for it. If you do not shampoo very often, it may be necessary to shampoo twice. The first round can be very short, up to a minute. After the shampoo binds with dust and debris, rinse right away, so you don't massage them back into the scalp. The second round can be two minutes long, and you can massage the shampoo into the scalp. Rinse for at least a minute with lukewarm water. You can feel the texture change to squeaky clean when the shampoo is completely gone. Finish with a cold brisk rinse to tighten the pores around each follicle reducing hair loss and creating more shine. If you cannot handle cold, make it as cool as you can stand.

If you shampoo every day, you can make the process much milder by shampooing only once and diluting your shampoo with filtered water. A mountain of foam will not make your hair cleaner. If your shampoo produces lots of lather, it may be due to unwanted sulfates. Too much 'air' from the foamy lather can create too much dryness.

Give your scalp an occasional soap break by skipping a day of shampooing, just rinse and condition or switch to one lathering only and do a two-round shampoo once a week or just once a month, depending on your hair.

Rotating or not rotating shampoos?

Both strategies can work. We have clients who use one simple product successfully for decades. Others get a better result from rotating formulas.

Too many people when showering put the shampoo on top of the head and then work the shampoo downward. This practice often touches only the hair surface and neglects the scalp underneath. This can result in buildup and dandruff.

You will want to separate the thicker, stronger hair in the middle of the back of the head, and apply the shampoo there. Then move upwards in a massaging motion towards the top, so that the more fragile 'umbrella' hair on the crown, receives less shampoo and less friction.

Unless we use a lot of styling products, our hair only collects some dust, sweat, and oil secretions at the most. To decrease shampoo mania it is important to realize that hair by itself is not dirty. Or course, if someone uses a lot of product, it is necessary to clean the build-up off the hair and scalp. Occasional use of a clarifying shampoo or lathering twice will generally clear any accumulation. Some people clean their hair as if it is a piece of cloth rather than a precious part of the body. That kind of treatment is too rough. Hair is not woven together like a fabric. Instead, it consists of thousands of single threads. Some hair is stronger and more resilient. People with fine, long, or chemically treated hair must care for their hair in a more conscious, gentle manner if they want to keep it healthy. It helps if we shift our focus from shampooing the hair to cleaning the scalp. Just wash your scalp. After the shampoo is massaged all over the scalp, the rinsing process will automatically spread the shampoo throughout the hair, cleaning it as it is being rinsed out.

How often to Shampoo

We have met people who had not washed their hair with soap for months or even a year and still maintained a clean and healthy scalp and hair with no unpleasant odors. They live very close to nature and would simply use water, vinegar or herb tinctures for rinsing hair. The scalp does have a self-regulating cleaning function and does not depend on soaps, especially when it is brushed regularly. These examples are not meant to set a standard, in fact they are quite rare. In our modern world, working environments, street dust, pollution, and styling products necessitate more frequent shampooing. We have also seen clients who have adopted the 'No-Poo' policy with their hair, sometimes replacing shampoo simply with baking soda. Some people believe it works for them, yet others accumulate a buildup of oil and dust that makes the hair look heavy and dull. This mostly depends on the water quality and the individual's unique chemistry. Using baking soda alone can make the hair too alkaline, when it would like to be slightly acidic. That is why baking soda should generally be mixed with organic apple cider vinegar.

If you shampoo every day or every other day and your hair is in great condition, you can trust you are doing the right thing. If your hair and scalp are dry, too oily, or itchy, it is a sign that your scalp is out of balance, and you might need to change your shampooing practice. Perhaps you shampoo too often, overuse shampoo each time, or you simply need a different product.

Most of us shampoo with too much lather and too often. The more lather, the more quickly we can cover the whole head of hair. We get used to feeling a lot of soap gliding over the head, associate it with cleanliness, and want to experience the fluffiness and lightness of fresh-washed hair all the time. The next day, when the sebaceous glands have been activated and the hair is weighed down with a small amount of natural oil, it may feel 'dirty' again. If the hair is washed every day, it keeps being stripped of its natural oils, which are essential for shiny, silky hair. The message the brain gets is that the scalp does not have enough oil, so it will often produce more. Here, short-term ease and convenience counteract the long-term goal of healthy hair.

According to market statistics, Americans, Canadians, and Europeans are shampooing more and more. This leads to scalp and hair problems that create a demand for restorative hair care products. When it comes to shampooing, our motto is: "Less is more." As many people age and less oil is produced, washing every five to seven days can be enough. This is where you must experiment to see what works best for your hair.

Conditioners

We are so 'conditioned' to use conditioners that we don't reflect and evaluate for ourselves if we really need them or if they are good for our hair in the long term. Virgin hair, meaning hair that is not chemically treated, rarely needs to be conditioned unless it is long and has become damaged by the environment, harsh shampoos or harmful practices.

Nature's simplest way of conditioning the hair is using cold water rinses. After shampooing your hair once or twice and rinsing out the soap with lukewarm water, finish with a cold rinse. This causes the hair cuticle to close, creating a protective shield. It also helps to keep the hair from getting tangled. Using warm water for the final rinse leaves the cuticle open and vulnerable to external damage. Cold-rinsed hair will appear shinier because the daylight reflects more fully on one homogeneous, smooth layer of cuticle. Another positive effect of the cold water rinse is improved blood circulation, and oxygen supply to the scalp. This nourishes the follicles, contributing to healthier hair. Increased circulation, as with brushing, will also feed your brain, eyes, ears, and skin. In addition, the volume of the hair will seem to increase as the cold water contracts the scalp, causing the hair shafts to stand up straight, creating more height and fullness. It might take a while to get used to the cold water, and you can bend in the shower to avoid the cold splashing on your body unless you are desiring a whole body cold rinse. Most people wash and rinse hair in the shower where it is very easy to target the cool rinse on just the head by bending forward or back. Remember, you can still enjoy hot water from the neck down, keeping your body nice and warm. The heat from your body will rise, warming your head on the inside so the cool rinse will not be as unpleasant as you might imagine. Once it has become a habit, you won't want to miss the invigorating experience or the healthy hair results.

The Golden Hair Tip

Rinsing your hair with clean cold water
is a very powerful hair care practice for:

1. Protecting the Hair's
   Strength and Longevity
2. Increasing Shine
3. Enhancing Color
4. Creating more Volume
5. Enlivening Energy
6. Boosting Circulation

Detanglers and conditioners help detangle long and curly hair and are very efficient for combing chemically treated hair. However, some conditioners create a vicious cycle by leaving a heavy coating that attracts dirt, creating the need for more frequent washing. This makes the hair even dryer. The more chemical ingredients that you apply to your hair, the more conditioning and repair products will seem necessary to restore it.

A good conditioner will contain essential fatty and amino acids that can strengthen the hair. Rosemary, sage, horsetail, and coltsfoot are herbs that contain these necessary elements. Natural herbal oils are also beneficial in restoring shine and resilience. If you condition your hair, try conditioning only the ends. Hair is oilier near the scalp and does not benefit from adding conditioner there. If you have longer hair, condition only the hair that can be put in a high ponytail, or hair from the earlobes down. Shampoo should concentrate on the scalp, conditioning should concentrate on the hair shaft.

When choosing a conditioner, again, use your nose. Do you like the smell? Use your eyes to see if the product is chemical-free especially avoiding mineral oil derivatives like propylene glycol.

Occasionally when we wash our client's hair, even after shampooing it twice, there is still conditioner left from the last time they applied it. This means, they used too much and could reduce the amount or use a lighter formula.

Hair Rinses and Moisturizing

Herbal rinses can replace shampoo or be applied after shampooing or conditioning. If your hair is dry a rinse is best before conditioning. For oily hair, use the herbal rinse as your last step. Prepare them by brewing herb teas, letting them cool, and then apply. Some of the best herbs for hair care are sage, rosemary, and chamomile. Chamomile lightens and softens the hair. You can combine rosemary and sage for dark hair or use them separately. The temperature of an herbal rinse can be lukewarm to cold. A cold herbal rinse can be added to your shampoo or applied afterwards. When you rinse your hair, catch the herb water with a bowl so you can use it right away several times. Basil brings shine especially to dark hair in combination with rosemary, and to blond hair in combination with chamomile. Nettle helps reduce oiliness of scalp and hair. Cold or lukewarm herb teas can also be mixed with sparkling mineral water. Indulge yourself occasionally with a final rinse of pure sparkling mineral water, which feels tingly and wonderful! If you live in a dry climate or work in an air-conditioned or heated environment, you can also moisturize your hair by spraying both your skin and hair with water or aloe vera diluted with water. You can purchase or make your own skin and hair toner. Find a small spray bottle at a drug or beauty supply store. Fill it with filtered or sparkling mineral water and add one or two drops of pure essential oil.

How to Put an End to Dry Ends

Many of our clients who are conscious of diet, water, and avoid chemicals in styling products wonder if they are doing something wrong when they notice that their ends are dry. Dry ends result from excessive heat, chemicals in hair products, chlorine and minerals in the water, and especially the weather!

- Spritz your hair and face when you drink water. Think rain and moisture for your hair.
- During winter months and in air-conditioned environments set up a humidifier.
- Protect your ends with a light bit of your chosen oil to seal the moisture in!
- If you drive a convertible or motorcycle secure your hair so it won't get thrashed in the wind.

The Magic of Aloe Vera

Pure aloe vera, either straight from the leaf or bottled is a fantastic natural conditioner. You can spray diluted aloe vera to enhance curl or reduce static or use it as a styling gel, which also conditions your hair and soothes an irritated scalp.

Fire – Energizing – Yang

Hair wants to be radiant and sparkle like fire. It needs sunlight for its growth and to assist the body in assimilating vitamin D. Yet too much fire will burn it. Excessive heat can be caused by 'chemical fire:' perms, straighteners, and coloring, and by too much 'electrical fire:' hot water, blow-drying, and straightening, and even environmental fire with saunas or too much sun.

Stimulating and Detoxifying

FROM THE INSIDE

Exercise sparks the element fire. Its two essential effects on hair and scalp are increased blood circulation and the elimination of toxins.

Inversion exercises contribute to hair health by causing blood to flow more easily to the scalp. Simply lean forward while brushing your hair, or just relax while putting your legs up against the wall or lying on a slant board.

The Yoga positions *Candle* and *Plough*, as well as head and shoulder stands all increase the blood circulation toward the scalp by inversion.

T'ai Chi movements that direct the flow of energy toward the head or disperse excess energy are also helpful. There are also exercises in Yoga and T'ai Chi that promote the health of a particular organ or body part, indirectly stimulating hair and scalp. Strengthening the major organs with enough nutrition and effective exercise allows the body to direct nutrition and energy to the luxury item, the hair.

Conscious Haircutting

Haircutting is an act that, if performed consciously, will graciously combine all the elements enhancing a person's overall balance and energy in addition to creating a beautiful style. The process of cutting hair is essentially aggressive, Yang, fiery. Combing and stroking the hair is feminine, gentle, and soothing, belonging to the Yin elements of Earth and Water.

Getting a conscious haircut is an essential part of holistic hair care because it renews, transforms, stimulates and refines our hair and us. A haircut does much more than shorten hairs and create a style. It can affect your entire energy system and sense of well being. An acupuncturist who has enjoyed

FROM THE OUTSIDE

Hair Balancing for many years, even comes for a balancing when her hair is still looking great, just for the healing benefits. She says it clears her energy field and feels like a new beginning. The research of a another acupuncturist concluded that one Hair Balancing session can have the healing effect of several acupuncture treatments. Hair Balancing has reduced or eliminated hair loss for many clients by relaxing tension in scalp muscles and increasing circulation. How your hair is cut may make a profound difference in the very first appointment and can have a dramatic impact over time.

Suggestions for a Positive Haircutting Experience

Communicating with your hairdresser

Clearly convey what you would like for your haircut. Be specific using a ruler, bringing photos if possible while maintaining eye contact, when you tell your hairdresser your wishes. Let the hairdresser know what your current styling routine is like and if you are open to change.

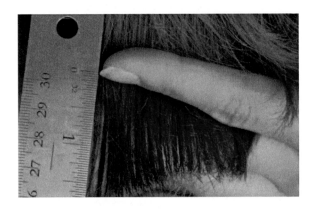

Many hairstyles involve some degree of layering and this is where precise communication is critical. Just looking at any current hairdressing magazine, one can see cuts where the layering is meant to be very obvious and even chunky. When someone wants layers, it is important to communicate what type and how much layering is desired or the results could be very disappointing. The most common layering would focus on the last few inches of the hair to create more movement and fun in the ends. You can tell the hairdresser to layer only the last two or three inches. Other common layering choices are to have them begin about chin length, earlobe, or around cheekbone length.

Another very effective form of layering, especially helpful to repair damage to the outer layers, is to do a very light layering to just the outer sections of hair that are most exposed to the elements. This also removes splits, breaks, and dry hairs from the most visible regions, revealing the healthier hairs underneath them. With fine hair this layering is done most carefully to maintain volume. People with very thick hair obviously have more leeway when it comes to layering. With a balanced haircut, the layering is usually very subtle and blended to the degree that when it is combed or brushed smooth it appears to be one length. When the hair is spritzed, scrunched or set with rollers to activate the waves and curls, the layers come alive with fullness.

Check your haircut before you leave. Even if the hairdresser has cut your hair for years, take a mirror and look at the finished result. See if there are any hairs hidden behind the ears or under very thick hair in the back or even trapped under the cape. Comb, brush, or use your fingers to bring your energy back into your hair and check that the hair falls into place the way you want it.

Bringing photos to your hair appointment

Sometimes a client will bring a photo of a desired style and it is not possible to create that style given certain realities. Most likely the model in the photograph could never get her hair to look like that again without stylists, fans, and a photographer who managed to get that one shot out of hundreds, supported by Photoshop.

Bringing a photo provides an excellent means to discuss what elements of the photo are most appealing, and what elements are possible. The conversation takes place before any cutting is done, so both parties have a realistic expectation of the outcome. The communication is as important as the cutting and styling. It is fundamental to achieving the right cut. It is helpful for the client or practitioner to say, for example, "What I think I hear you saying is, the light layering will begin at around the jaw line, is that correct?"

This communication is essential if this is the first appointment, and especially if a new style is requested. Being certain that you and your hair stylist are describing the same thing, is like a familiar saying in carpentry, "measure twice and cut once."

Sunshine

The sun is the ultimate source of energy. Considering the season, location and your personal tolerance to sun exposure, experiment with absorbing the healing energy of the sun, charging yourself and your hair. In general, do not sunbathe longer than thirty minutes and not between 11 AM and 2 PM. To receive the daily needed dosage of vitamin D, 20% of the skin's surface needs to be exposed to the sun for 30 minutes at a location near sea level. Face and hands only make up 5% of the skin's surface. Balance sunbathing by drinking more water, and by applying a moist cloth to your skin or spritzing water.

If your hair is thinning or you have bald spots, watch your exposure to the sun to avoid burns on the scalp. If the skin damage is deep, it can affect the hair roots. Organic, chemical free sun blocks can be used for the scalp. Hats are great.

Sunlight will lighten hair color. In combination with seawater or lemon juice or chamomile, it can create beautiful streaks of different highlights. Saltwater does not create highlights by itself, only in combination with sunlight. Herbs and plants like chamomile and rhubarb have highlighting effects, but need to be applied quite frequently to be noticeable. The beauty industry has created chemical products that imitate natural highlights. Yet, whether the sun or chemicals create highlights, highlighted hair is drier and more prone to breakage.

If you want to protect your hair from damage or natural highlights while visiting the beach, swimming in the ocean or enjoying outdoor sports, the best advice is cover your head. Hair reacts very differently to various climates and needs some time to adapt just as our bodies and psyches do. Some people experience that heat makes their hair swell and humidity encourages curls. Others find heat and humidity make their hair simply limp. Understand how your hair responds so you can give it the care it needs in different environments.

> **What if I want to dispose of my cut hair in a special way?**
>
> Occasionally, the cut hair seems to carry an energy that needs special transformation. It feels heavy to the client or us and the question arises, should it be burnt, buried, or thrown away? In those cases, we prefer using the fire element to assist in a quick transformation. If your intuition prompts you to do something different with the hair, follow it.

Decrease Hot Water

Frequent use of hot water weakens the scalp's immune system. We want to emphasize again that it causes the muscle tissue surrounding the follicles to relax. Consequently, the follicles expand, having less hold on the hair, causing hair to simply fall out. If you are experiencing hair loss, switch immediately from hot to lukewarm or cool water for washing and conditioning, then finish with cold rinses. This one change can make a rapid and substantial difference in the amount of hair lost.

Reduce Use of Electric Styling Tools

Next time after your hair is cut, feel the cut pieces on the floor, then touch the ends of the hair on your head with the other hand. The cut pieces will usually feel drier. Often they are more damaged, but even if not, hair changes electric polarity as soon as it is cut and becomes positively charged. The hair on the head keeps a negative charge, which is good, unless it has been repeatedly treated with chemicals.

Blow-drying is a combination of the elements Air and Fire. It not only dries the hair, but can actually fry it. The same is true for electric curlers, curling irons and flat irons. Dry hair can become static when combed or brushed, even making sparking sounds. Plastic tools increase the static. Wooden or rubber combs reduce the fireworks on your head. Wetting your combs and brushes also helps to decrease static.

Chemicals

For people with chemically treated hair, please note that the following passage is not meant to create fear or insecurity or to be judgmental. The intention is to inform, especially in the sense of enhancing and maintaining the health of scalp and hair. There are always personal exceptions. If chemically induced colors and waves give you joy or freedom, it is possible that within the context of your whole self, the negative consequences on your system are minimal.

Chemicals are not always bad, but some, if applied and absorbed into your body, can compromise the health of your hair, scalp, and body. Some hair can handle chemical treatments better than others. One permanent wave will not necessarily completely destroy your hair, but sometimes the damage is so great it requires cutting off all the permed hair. Laura experienced this horrifying result from what was supposed to be just a light body wave. Be aware as there is always a risk. This is because a perm changes the molecular structure of your hair. The more chemicals you use, the more harm is done. The result of most chemical treatments is drier hair. Coloring the hair is not as aggressive as perming it, because the color only penetrates or coats the hair shaft and does not rearrange the molecules. Chemical hair coloring still damages the hair shaft and can enter the body through the scalp. Semi-permanent coloring formulas, known as level 2, have no ammonia and lower levels of peroxide. They fade gradually over 12-28 washings. Less harmful varieties only coat the hair and wash out after a few weeks. Bleaching will strip the color molecules from the hair. Since the chemically opened cuticle makes each hair rougher and appear thicker, some hairdressers use this side effect of bleaching to create the effect of more volume. It works for that aspect, but eventually the hair loses shine and vitality and breaks more easily.

Regarding the effect of chemicals on the inside, whatever you put on the scalp is absorbed within two to three minutes and can be traced in the bloodstream. Whenever you receive a chemical hair treatment, your scalp is drinking a tiny portion of the chemical solution. Some main ingredients of hair dyes are known to cause cancer, and there have been links with hair dyes and Non-Hodgkin's Lymphoma. In addition, chemicals in hair products add to the pollution of our planet as they wash down our drains damaging the waters and other life forms.

Highlights and hair dyes are often applied straight onto the scalp, to postpone the appearance of the original color. Although you may have to color your hair more often, it is definitely healthier to avoid coloring down to the roots, thus minimizing absorption into the scalp.

Several research studies published in the last five years do not relate coloring and perming to the development of cancer and seem to ease the consumer's mind. We have to consider who finances these studies and question the validity of the tests themselves. Carcinogens derived from chemical hair treatments might have a more dangerous effect when used for a much longer period of time than these tests covered. When the epidemiological studies include women who have used hair dyes for more then two decades, the correlation with different types of cancer increases drastically. Many women start using chemical hair dyes, straighteners, and perms when they are teenagers. In their thirties, decades of coloring, straightening, and perming may have cumulatively weakened their immune system.

Even if none of the women using hair dyes over the test period developed significantly more cancer than women who didn't use color, this does not prove that chemicals are not having an effect. Known carcinogens are found in temporary, semi-permanent, and permanent dyes.

In addition, some hair coloring products contain lead. Since companies don't have to list heavy metals as ingredients, the consumer can unknowingly be exposed to them as well. You may recall that exposure to lead caused brain damage in the ruling class of the Roman Empire prior to its collapse. Some advertisements claim 'No ammonia' or 'No peroxide.' This might be true and is positive, but other harmful chemicals often replace the ones the consumer is trying to avoid. One solution is to expose the box of hair color to an energy transformation device. This can reverse the polarity on the toxic ingredients making it difficult for them to attach to the body.

Fortunately, a growing part of the hair care industry is busy developing less toxic hair colors based on plant ingredients. Chamomile, rhubarb, sage, black walnut, coffee, and, the best known one, henna, are creating safer coloring results for your hair. If you are currently using chemical hair coloring products, consider asking your hair stylist to assist you in making the transition to more gentle or natural hair coloring products. One must consider if an action or substance raises or diminishes their vibration and make choices accordingly.

During Pregnancy and other Special Conditions

If you are pregnant or breast feeding, have hair loss or scalp problems, suffer from any chronic illness or if you have a family history of cancer or immune deficiency,  we suggest you refrain from chemical hair treatments. It is a general practice in hair salons to discourage pregnant women from coloring or perming their hair. One reason is that the hair of a pregnant woman or a woman on her moon will sometimes not take or hold a perm due to hormonal changes. Hairdressers want to avoid disappointment. Our main concern is that chemical exposure can reach the fetus through the bloodstream.

Chemical-free Perms Don't Exist

To our knowledge, there are no permanent waves or straighteners that are chemical-free. Manufacturers add the words natural, bio, and organic to give the impression that their product is a healthier. Only chemical manipulation altering the molecular structure of hair can guarantee long term curl or straightening. Perms labeled as 'natural' usually have enzymes, vitamins, and essential oils added to the chemicals. These additions reduce the harshness and odor of conventional perm products. If you choose to have a perm, we recommend researching the product and its application to determine its quality. This can save you from hair disasters that end up costing more money, time, and trouble.

Invigoration

In modest amounts, fiery ingredients and remedies are chosen to invigorate scalp and hair and stimulate new hair growth. Ginger, cayenne pepper, and organic apple cider vinegar are just a few options from the healthy hair pharmacy. All these give skin and scalp a slight burning.

Ginger for Your Roots

China's #1 hair loss remedy can be used as a spice, a tea, a supplement, a rinse or applied straight onto the scalp. Cut a ginger root diagonally into slices to maximize exposed surfaces and rub them straight onto your scalp or steep in boiling water for a tea or rinse.

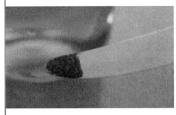

The Cayenne Treatment

To stimulate the roots of your hair and your scalp dip the tip of a knife into cayenne powder, then mix it with one tablespoon of cold-pressed olive oil. Massage it onto your scalp. To increase the power of this treatment, go into the sauna or steam with your hot dressing on.

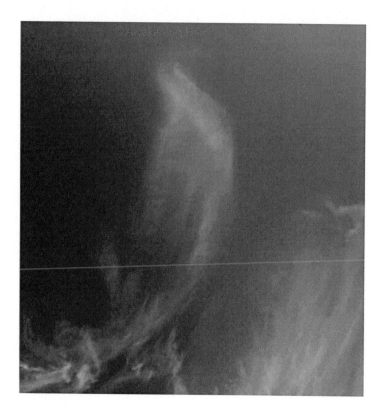

Air – Expanding – Yang

The ideal hairstyle is aerodynamic, meaning the hair moves freely through space. When you brush your hair and then shake it, you should feel the hair's liberated movement.

Breathing for Your Hair

The breath is the carrier of life energy and ultimately nourishes our hair. Breathe into your hair and imagine the breath going all the way up into the roots and flowing out through the ends of the hair.

When you receive a haircut watch your breathing and make sure that you don't hold your breath. Many people replace deep breaths with shallow breathing while receiving or giving a haircut. During childhood we were told to "stay still," and "don't move," thus, as children, we held our breath. Of course, it is important to be still so we can avoid accidents with scissors and receive an even haircut. Continue breathing, even if the hairdresser is very close with his or her scissors. We receive more of the overall benefit of the haircut, when we relax and breathe calmly.

Air-drying

Air is the first choice for drying freshly washed hair. Air-drying means letting the hair dry indoors or outdoors by the normal or moderate temperature of your home and climate making sure to avoid over-exposure to sun and wind.

Towel-drying

After you have washed your hair, if you have longer hair gently press excess water out in the shower, then wrap a dry towel around your head and press. A second towel is necessary because the towel you just used for drying your body won't absorb much water anymore. Don't rub hair that is longer than four inches. The concept of making fire by rubbing two sticks together, or rubbing hands to create warmth, does not work for drying hair. Hair consists of many fine strands that can break when rubbed harshly. Pressing hair in between the towel or pressing the towel against the scalp soaks up the water easily, and you can simply take another dry towel and repeat the process. Cotton towels usually work best, although certain microfibers have been developed for greater absorbency, and have less weight and bulk.

Depending on the length of your hair, you may even use a third towel. The last towel can be kept on for a little while longer to help the scalp and hair warm from inside using the body's heat. Terrycloth turbans designed for drying hair are less bulky and do not easily fall off. After a few minutes, remove the towel or turban, work in some leave-in conditioner or a touch of oil if you use it, finger comb, and let your hair air-dry. You may comb and style the hair, when it is at least two-thirds dry. If we comb or brush wet hair, we stretch it, which decreases its elasticity.

Blow-drying

When you finish blow-drying your hair, if it is completely dry, it has been dried too much. People who choose to blow-dry should leave the hair shaft, not the roots, just a little bit damp. It will air dry very quickly.

Many people blow-dry their hair to add volume. Once they get used to the light and fluffy feeling, they dislike the feeling of un-blown hair or even experience stress when they don't blow-dry. Reducing the heat and shortening the drying time are easy steps you can take towards healthier hair.

The choice of blow dryer can be important. There are various kinds of dryers, which create different types of heat, which are more or less damaging. The less heat, the better for your hair and scalp. Although there is no such thing as a healthy dryer, we found three qualities to make them less objectionable:

1. the use of negative ions while drying, which leaves the hair surprisingly soft and manageable.
2. technology reducing electromagnetic disturbance
3. technology which reduces noise, a relief from the usual noise pollution hair dryers make.

Manufacturers will feature these qualities on the box and in their advertising.

Does everyone have more hair on one side than the other?

The asymmetry of humanness manifests in hair as well. There are always more hairs on one side of the head than the other. We all have one thicker side and one with not quite as much hair. Another way each side is different, is that the flow of the hair is influenced by the whorl, which creates one side flowing forward more easily while the opposite side flows more effortlessly toward the back. This is why so many people struggle when trying to achieve symmetry with a hairstyle. Ideally, we understand and integrate the asymmetry of nature as it expresses through hair.

Hair Volume

You can increase or decrease hair volume by:
• Brushing the roots forward and then backward.
The strokes forward can add volume, and the strokes backward create a more finished look.
• Using combs, clips, and ties to give the hair a lift while it is drying after spritzing or washing the hair. Lifting the roots away from the scalp keeps hair cleaner longer. Lifting the hair at night, can make the hair appear much fuller during the day. Sleeping with hair down tends to flatten it.
• Hair care products that are more drying than moisturizing can create the appearance of more volume. The principle is that water, moisturizers, and oils weigh the hair down; air lifts it up. For some people with curly or wavy hair, more moisture will encourage the curls to become stronger, which can result in more volume. Again, know your hair.
• The cold-water rinse adds volume, while hot water flattens the hair. Even if you want flat, smooth hair, avoid the hot water because in the long run it dries out and dulls the hair shaft. It is better to brush your hair and let the oil of your sebaceous glands smooth and add shine to your hair.

False Depictions of Hair in Advertising

Most advertising agencies and stylists for commercials choose to enhance the model's hair regardless of the product. Beautiful hair equals sexual attraction and sex sells.

Wigs, weaves, and extensions from real and synthetic hair, chemical products, special lighting, and of course Photo Shop, are all used to create hair that looks 'Super Shiny,' 'Super Flowing,' 'Perfectly Smooth,' 'Extra Voluminous.'

Don't compare your hair to FAKE HAIR. Don't indulge feelings of inadequacy by comparing your hair to hair that is not real. Don't allow yourself to be manipulated by false images designed to make you buy products hoping you can achieve this false perfection. Hair that appears to be long and all one length is often achieved with fake hair. The models in the ads do not really look like they appear in the photos. Styling is after all an industry in itself.

Head Covers and Wigs

Two thirds of the earth's women wear head covers for protection, religious reasons, or fashion. Some head covers can put a lot of strain on the head, resulting in headaches and tension. Many hat designs, including those for work or sports requirements like helmets and bathing caps, press on the arteries and veins along the scalp. This inhibits the free flow of blood and oxygen to the roots of the hair. If head covers are not made out of cotton or breathable materials, they can cause scalp disorders such as dandruff and hair loss, because the heightened temperature and lack of ventilation provide a breeding ground for bacteria. One solution for helmet wearers is to put a silk cap or scarf between your hair and the inside of the helmet.

Wigs and hairpieces are often used to cover balding or thinning hair. They are a solution for the visual disadvantages hair loss creates, or they can satisfy expressive needs, personally or professionally. If wigs are used on a regular or even daily basis, they might cause the same hair problems that occur with head covers. Hair and scalp need air and light. If you wear a wig, make sure that you air out your head as often as possible and expose it to daylight. Air out the wig as well.

Wigs and hairpieces are made of human, animal, or synthetic hair. The base of a wig or hairpiece is usually made out of plastic. Most of them have lace fronts that help with ventilation. Having this additional material on the scalp increases heat. On top of the normal hair, it can be like wearing a woolen hat indoors. If you choose a wig made of human hair, consider clearing it energetically as hair holds energy from its original source.

If you feel that a wig or hairpiece helps you achieve your desired effect, shop around and look for quality work.

Ballerinas and other performers often put their hair up very tightly, which over time can cause the hairline to recede due to tension on the front hairs. Even worse, the hair is slicked back with hair spray and often covered with wigs. If you prefer your hair covered, fastened tightly, or pulled back most of the time, all the previous ideas for creating volume would be great for achieving more balance. Hair needs to breathe and fly freely at least occasionally.

Split Hair Prevention

Hair can split or break due to chemical damage, nutritional imbalances, drying ingredients in hair products, stress, environmental conditions, toxicity, climate, poor quality combs and brushes, and certain fabrics rubbed against the hair. Hair splits when the cuticle layer has too much air, is too dry, and not lubricated enough.

A lot of movement while sleeping on a synthetic pillowcase can contribute to hair breakage. Very high thread count cotton, silk and satin pillow covers are definitely friendlier materials. Braiding long hair for sleeping or securing it on top of the head can be helpful in minimizing splits.

The quality of hair ties and accessories is important. Cotton, silk, and leather harmonize with hair better than most plastic and metal, and cause less friction. Check any 'hair holder' or barrette for rough or sharp edges or seams.

If you always secure your hair in the same place, your hair may tend to break along that weakened area. Move that spot around a bit and let your hair fly free occasionally.

A split hair is like a dry branch cracked open into two or more parts. It cannot be mended together. It can be filled and that is what some conditioners do, but it does not grow back together. There are only two solutions for split hair: cutting and prevention. Commercial split end repair products are fillers, which only last a limited time, and their residue often causes more dryness and breakage. Some split end repair products can postpone dry hair from breaking with the help of an external lubricating treatment. This might be helpful for the short term, but it is prolonging the condition rather than curing it.

A head of virgin hair is rarely full of split ends. Usually, there is more healthy hair than split hair. Interestingly, we hear our clients say that they have lots of split ends, yet when we look for them, there are hardly any split hairs to be found.

Many women think their hair is split when it is only dry or has many different lengths. Discovering hair of different lengths does not necessarily mean it has broken. Hairs may just be at their natural stages in the hair growth cycle or it could be the result of a previous haircut.

Most split hair occurs at the ends of long hair or the crown hair, which grows from the highest part of the head. It becomes the outermost layers and more subject to damage. The crown hair is most exposed to climate influences and manipulative hair styling. When you have split hair and you are not attached to the length, the easiest way to solve the problem is by getting a very good haircut to remove the damage.

Part of the Hair Balancing method specializes in removing the damaged hair while retaining the maximum amount of length. Healthy hairs do not need to be sacrificed to remove the damaged hair.

From this point forward, you can start over with new hair care habits and dietary improvements. High acidity in the system through the consumption of too much 'sweet, meat, wheat' and even coffee may be contributing to split ends. If you want to grow your hair long, yet it breaks off at a certain length, a split hair repair job is essential. This means finding a hairdresser who can see the split ends and is willing to take the time to trim these damaged areas. The process can be made easier by taking small sections of hair, twisting them gently causing the split hairs to stick out. It is a tedious job and can strain the arms and eyes.

If the desire is to grow the hair healthier and longer, it is necessary to bring the whole head of hair beyond its 'breaking point'

Split End Prevention Summary

- Getting the split ends cut by a professional who will take the time to do a split end surgery without shortening the rest of the hair
- The split ends need to be cut 1/3 - 1/2 of an inch above the area where they split since that part of the hair is likely to split as well
- Using gentle hair bands
- Reducing exposure to heat: hot water, blow-drying, and sun
- Avoiding chemicals
- Brushing and oiling your hair
- Reducing acidic foods

Why does my hair not grow past a certain point?

Some people have the experience that their hair will not grow past a certain point. There are many reasons why this may be happening, and some interesting solutions.

Certain individuals have acquired a psychological barrier to long hair. We have worked with clients who were told during their childhood that their hair is not capable of growing long and that long hair will never be an option. Others were not allowed to grow long hair because in their family it represented something unwanted like an expression of femininity, sexuality, or rebellion, or was simply too much work for the parents. Mentally recalling and releasing the unwanted beliefs and accompanying patterns and welcoming the hair to finally grow, can heal these psychological blocks.

For some people there is actually a genetic barrier. To deal with this cause, serious mind over matter exercises plus an increased health regimen focusing on diet can be helpful. Remember only 30% of our physical conditions are due to genetics and we can often overcome these limitations. One of the main causes is breakage. If the scissors are dull or the cutting technique is too invasive the hair shaft gets ripped and is subject to splits and breaks. If the hair is cut too frequently and not nurtured beyond its usual breaking and length point through meticulous care, it will tend to stay at a certain length.

Hair can break due to weakness that is sourced by insufficient minerals, oils and vitamins in the diet. Attending to these dietary needs can strengthen hair so it is capable of sustaining new length.

According to yogic beliefs, every person's hair grows to a certain point and then if it is not cut, the energy and nutrients, which are producing new hair can be used for other physical or mental functions, such as meditation. It is up to the individual to assess what might be causing their situation and experiment with appropriate solutions.

YOUR HAIR CARE
IMPROVEMENT PLAN

Create your Hair Care Improvement Plan by using the following overview as your confirmation and action guide. Confirm with a check mark and plan action with an exclamation mark.

Earth - Nurturing - Yin

From the Inside
    Eating Well for Your Hair
From the Outside
    The Right Shampoo
    Organic Apple Cider Vinegar
    Oil Treatments
    Brushing
    Combing
    Massaging the Scalp
    Intuitive Pressure Points
    Scalp Scrubbing
    Pulling the Hair with a Fist

Water - Refreshing – Yin

From the Inside
    Drinking Well for Your Hair
From the Outside
    Natural, Filtered, Enlivened, or Bottled Water
    How to Shampoo
    How Often to Shampoo
    Shampoo
    Conditioners
    Hair Rinses and Moisturizers

Fire - Energizing – Yang

From the Inside
    Exercising for Your Hair
From the Outside
    Conscious Haircutting
    Sunshine
    Decrease Hot Water
    Reduce Use of Electric Styling Tools
    Chemicals
    Invigoration

Air - Expanding - Yang

From the Inside
    Breathing for Your Hair
From the Outside
    Air-Drying
    Towel-Drying
    Blow-Drying
    Hair Volume
    Head Covers and Wigs
    Split Hair Prevention

Congratulations for every check mark you made. Each one is a milestone on your path to vibrant hair. If you want more of these essential building blocks, the next step is to begin turning the exclamation marks into check marks.

Increase your motivation by becoming clear about what you want to achieve, why, and how. On the next page or on a separate piece of paper describe the length, style, quality, and image of your desired hair.

My Hair Care Improvement Plan

• Envision and describe the hair you wish to attain:

_____

_____

_____

• Write down your most important reasons and feelings.
This is why I want to achieve this result and how I will feel:

_____

_____

_____

• These are the holistic hair care activities I commit myself
to that will bring me closer to my goals:

I can act now and do…
I can balance … with…
I can change …
I will now incorporate … daily, weekly, monthly
I will reduce…
I will eliminate…
I will allow more time to…

You are likely to notice an improvement very soon, even
after a few days. For a major improvement please allow 90
days. Take a photo of your hair before you start and then
after three months. The results will delight you.

Spring Hair

Merrily poking through the soil.
Tender buds, fine hair.
Colors and forms are dancing.
Unlimited power to grow.
Hair wants to play.

SUN AND MOON CYCLES
AND YOUR HAIR

Our hair is brought to life not only through the power of nature's elements but also through the power of nature's rhythms. Hair grows, moves, changes, and heals in its own rhythms. At the same time, it is part of larger rhythms pulsing through the human body, the earth, the solar system, and the universe. The two rhythmic cycles that result from our earth circling around the sun and the moon circling around the earth also influence our hair and can fine-tune its care.

The Sun Cycle

The sun gives us the light to live. The sun determines our 24 hour cycle of day and night. Beyond the daily cycle, the sun determines our seasons. It takes the earth 365 1/4 days to circle the sun. The earth's axis is tilted at an angle of 23.5 degrees, causing our seasons. When the North Pole is closer to the sun, the northern half of the globe experiences summer and the southern half winter. When the North Pole is farther away from the sun, the northern half experiences winter and the southern half summer.

In the northern hemisphere, spring starts in late March with the vernal equinox, a day when day and night are of equal length. The autumnal equinox is six months later, at the end of September. Summer Solstice in late June is the longest day of the year and the beginning summer.

Summer Hair

Sun-bleached, bright, and full.
Sometimes sticky or sweaty.
Enjoys cold living water.
Floats in the ocean like love.
Dries in a breeze.

Six months later, winter begins with Winter Solstice, the shortest day and the longest night of the year.

The four seasons affect all life on this planet, including our hair. We keep our hair throughout most of our lifetime, unlike deciduous plants and trees, which change color with every season, and every autumn they lose their leaves. If humans lost their hair every autumn, no one would ever grow long hair.

Human hair cycles are more individual and more like the evergreen trees in that we keep our foliage for years.

Similar to trees and plants, most people experience their hair growing more slowly in the winter and find it growing faster in warm weather. The change of climates, locations, the pace of modern lifestyles, and personal conditions sometimes interrupt the collective rhythm and traditional cycles.

See how your hair is connected with the seasons and observe how your hair changes throughout the year. The most auspicious, rhythmic times of the year to cut your hair are near the winter and summer solstice and the spring and autumn equinox. You could choose these seasonal prime times and if desired, perhaps an additional haircut in between. Going short or even shaving the hair is most advisable in the beginning of spring when the forces of nature are rising, and on into the summer, when it is the warmest.

Autumn Hair

Hair celebrating abundance
before calming down,
preparing for transition and change.
Energy glowing from within,
as hairs surrender thankfully, crowning the earth.

The Moon Cycle

The moon reflects the sun and through magnetism, gravity, and magic, influences our life in numerous ways.

It takes the moon twenty-eight and a half days to revolve around the earth and the same time to rotate on its axis. We see only one side of the moon from our earthly perspective. The side we never see is called the dark moon, whereas the new moon is commonly called the black moon. The new moon occurs when the moon is between sun and earth, so the sunlight falls on it, but only the moon's shadow falls upon the earth. The time between the new moon and full moon is the waxing phase. The moon becomes fuller as the right side is increasingly bathed in light. The full moon occurs when the earth is between sun and moon. We see the sun shining fully onto the moon's surface. The moon is in the spotlight, and the earth is in the tension field between sun and moon. Therefore, it makes sense that the full moon time is more intense than the new moon time. The night becomes more like the day, and that additional light stimulates ovulation, births, emotions, romance, sexuality, growth cycles, appetite, and even criminal activities.

The time between full moon and new moon is the waning phase, and it is the left side of the moon which becomes crescent shaped. The new moon to full moon period is favorable for the beginning of projects, whereas the full moon to new moon period is suited more for strengthening and reworking or letting things go. Regarding hair, the waxing period supports faster, possibly thicker hair growth, and the waning period is for strengthening the hair from within. If you would like to integrate the lunar cycle into your life, begin with your personal experience: watch the moon wax, becoming fuller, and wane, going toward the new moon, every night. Or watch the influence of the moon on the tides. This will develop your sense of its rhythm and power. Reach out for the moon with its cool moon magic!

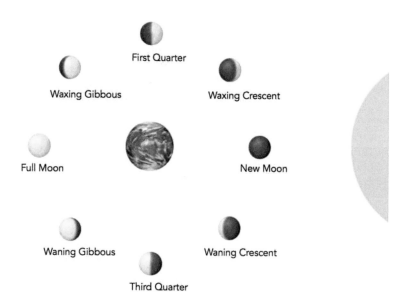

First Quarter

Waxing Gibbous

Waxing Crescent

Full Moon

New Moon

Waning Gibbous

Waning Crescent

Third Quarter

Some farmers and gardeners use the lunar cycle when they plant and prune their crops. Collective experience over centuries has shown that the phases of the moon influence the oceans as well as emotions, plant life, and hair growth.

You can use the lunar cycle and astrology as a guide and a way to be in tune with nature and right timing.

We and some of our clients experience the lunar connection to our head and hair as calming and healing. By cutting hair in harmony with the moon, we transfer the knowledge and influence of lunar gardening to our hair.

The Farmer's Almanac considers the seasons, the moon cycles, and the astrological signs that the sun and moon are in, to improve the results of planting crops. These influences can also stimulate new hair growth and strength, which represents maintaining and stimulating existing hair, and harvesting, which translates into pruning hair for health and volume. There are a number of favorable haircutting days each month depending on what results are desired. We sometimes use lunar cycle dates especially for clients who experience hair thinning. These dates can be refined even further by using an individual's natal astrological chart.

Moon Affirmation

As the moon grows full,
so does my hair.
While the moon is waning,
my hair gathers strength from within.
…and then the cycle starts again…

Winter Hair

Winter comes and covers the ground.
Hair is long and dark and warm.
Leaves disappear, but roots live on.
Hair curls around fingers
and takes you inside.

It can be helpful to use astrology in planning a visit to the hairdresser, dentist, or for a business trip. However, becoming dependent on this tool defeats the overall importance of tuning in and following one's intuition. Ultimately, choosing to attune to nature's cycles and using its rhythms to our advantage is about enhancing the quality of our lives.

If you do not relate to astrology, perhaps you will like this statement: The moon is always full.

And above all, trust your intuition.

Drinking Moonlight

People absorb the moon's energy simply
by being exposed to its light or gazing at it.
Try this powerful exercise:
Stand outdoors so you can see the moon.
Let your arms relax or place your hands on
top of the kidneys to keep your life force within.
Then breathe through your open mouth and while
inhaling, drink the cooling, calming, and
rejuvenating moonlight.
Guide your breath to the parts of your body that
need healing including scalp and hair.
Continue this breath for three minutes.

FIVE EASY STEPS
TO SUSTAINABLE HAIR CARE

Hair as the microcosmic mirror of the macrocosmic earth reflects the state of our planet. From one perspective we can see our hair and our planet chemically damaged, depleted, and out of balance. On the positive side, our hair and our planet are natural, wild, strong, beautiful, and resilient, having their own intelligence as they continue to grow. The leaves of the trees suffer from extreme climates just like our hair. Environmental pollution or acid rain falls upon leaves, the hairs of the trees. The use of hair spray for several decades has contributed to the holes in the ozone layer, increasing the harshness of our friend, the sun.

What is the long-term effect of hairspray on our hair, skin, and lungs?

What are the effects of perms and dyes on our body and environment?

What effect are chemicals having on our water supply, the fish, the algae, ultimately ourselves?

Where does the chemically processed hair go?

What does blow-drying cost the environment, my hair, and body?

Every action has a consequence and ignoring them doesn't make them go away. You can be part of sustainable hair care and contribute to your own and other people's health while still feeling and looking great.

Haircutting Outdoors

It is a very special experience to have your hair cut in nature: on the beach, on a mountaintop, in the middle of an extinct crater, in a cave or in the garden.
Where would you like to have your hair cut while absorbing the energies of nature?

STEP 1: RESEARCH

- Read and understand labels.
- Select hair and food products from conscious organic sources.
- Find hair care professionals who care for hair in a healthy, life-enhancing manner.

STEP 2: REPLACE

- Commercial styling aids and hair care products with life-enhancing, holistic alternatives.
- Substitute hair spray and commercial gels with aloe vera or lemon juice.
- Use conditioners with natural conditioning ingredients and cold water rinses.
- Instead of perms use rollers to curl your hair.
- Replace chemical straighteners with a straightening iron for special occasions.

STEP 3: REDUCE

- Reduce our exposure to chemical coloring with natural plant colors such as henna, coffee, sage, rhubarb and chamomile.
- Color your hair less often.
- Shampoo less often and with smaller amounts.

STEP 4: RECYCLE

• Recycle empty product bottles made out of glass, plastic, and aluminum and support companies that refill bottles.

• Recycle unwanted personal care products by donating them to homeless shelters.

• Every day a lot of cut hair is discarded all around the world, landing in the garbage. Here are three good uses for cut hair:

- Cut hair can be pressed into mats, which absorb oil spills. Search the internet for organizations doing this.

- Donate longer pieces of hair to organizations making wigs for sick children and cancer patients. The internet has links to these organizations.

- Hair for your garden! Although hair does not disintegrate quickly, its richness and energy can add growing power to the garden. Buried in the perimeter it can dissuade unwanted varmints from invading the garden. The nitrogen of cut hair fertilizes the soil.

STEP 5: REMEMBER

• You and your hair are beautiful. There is nothing fundamentally wrong that can not be remedied by nature. If there were something severely out of balance, you would need more than a fancy new chemical product or styling tool. Chances are that you can take care of slight imbalances with simple measures.

Hair in the Light

The Earth vibrates and radiates in the light of love.
The light workers abound.
All beings who are giving their energy to the healing of
the planet are connected through bonds of light
strengthening the shield of Mother Earth.

People are free and divine.
Every woman, every man, every child is uplifted
to be the queen and the king
crowned with luminous hair.
Every person wears their natural adornment
in dignity and beauty.

Their hair is light like the new vibration,
and free like their spirits.
Hair is flying and shining
as the life energy flows through the whole person
and the aura expands into the infinite.
Hair is in harmony with body, mind, and soul.
Hair is in balance and at one with nature.

People all over the planet
are bridges connecting Heaven and Earth.
Their hair reaches out as antennae to the sky
at the same time rooted firmly to the ground.

The Earth is laughing.
Nature is vibrating in joy.
All colors are shimmering.
All tones are sounding
and the entire creation is celebrating.
People are dancing and loving
as their hair swings and sparkles in the light.

HAIR IN THE LIGHT

The destinies of humanity are woven together with threads of hair. We are all connected with one another. We are a family of hair; souls who have come to live on planet Earth to learn and experience wisdom, love, balance, and polarity. Earth is a cosmic hair and energy garden. If we bring light to the aspect of hair, the ripple effect can reach far into our universe. As we heal our hair, we heal ourselves, and we heal the planet.

Your hair loves you and is part of you. Your hair will always want to please you. If there is something it needs, it will let you know. Check in once in a while. Experiment, experience, fine tune, and share. You each leave a hair legacy behind.

We have built machines and created medications that prolong our lives, and we use chemicals that give our hair the color it once had. If there were no hair color treatments available, we would see lots of white haired people everywhere. The natural diversity of hair colors on this planet would unite into the global white hair of all races toward the end of our lives.

The future of hair is already here. The holistic hair care movement is creating hairstyles with a focus on health, balance, and natural beauty. When the awareness of chakras, acupuncture meridians, and sacred geometry has become part of our cultural wisdom, hair that is energetically cut and matched to each individual person will be an accepted and preferred part of life. In the not too distant future, Hair Balancing will be a commonplace healing and grooming experience. Energy-efficient hairstyles will beautify and strengthen the individual. Perhaps our telepathic and mental abilities will evolve to where we can create and manipulate our outer appearance at will. Or could we develop hair that is able to overcome gravity and energetically feel, heal, and caress its surroundings, like the Navi people in Avatar? Who knows?

More people are discovering that external beauty is just one aspect of how we experience our hair. We can also perceive the radiance sourced from within connecting harmoniously with everything around us.

Awaken to the new life and beauty that is possible.

Awaken the   for Your Hair
Love
There is one piece of advice, which

will work for thousands of people

and every type of hair, which

is love the hair you have

and it becomes

the hair you

love.

Laura Sullivan & Linda Deslauriers

Epilogue

You can see hair in the light especially well in the morning and evening hours. When the sunlight falls onto the leaves and brightens them up, look out for children who play in the park or people taking a walk on the beach to gaze at the amazing backlighting effect on the hair.

Search for that moment when the lighting is just perfect. All the hair merges and dissolves in the light. Hair is one unit. The hair transforms the sunlight into a diffuse corona that softly touches the viewer. Hair in the light is one of the most beautiful, wondrous, and magical phenomena on this earth.

INGREDIENT ALERT GUIDE

If you don't like reading labels, find the print too small, or think the long Latin names are too confusing, check this list of the commonly used ingredients that are most important for you to avoid for your general health and well being, and of course the ultimate beauty of your hair. The main ingredients to avoid are

Detergents
Petroleum derivatives
Artificial colors and fragrances.

Detergents are designed to create suds for cutting through heavy grease, which we mistake for cleaning ability. Unfortunately, most sudsing ingredients strip the hair of its needed natural oils. This makes for dry, fly away, dull or lifeless hair creating a need for conditioners. Some of the most common names for detergents include; sodium lauryl sulfate, sodium laureth sulfate, sodium myreth sulfate, and sodium olefin sulfate. These and other sodium sulfates can be irritating to skin and eyes, sometimes causing rashes, hair loss, flaking and allergic reactions.

Propylene Glycol is one of the most widely used cosmetic ingredients. It absorbs moisture, acts as a solvent and emollient. It can cause allergic and toxic reactions. Industrial size containers of propylene glycol have warnings to avoid contact with skin.

Petroleum derivatives such as methyl, propyl, butyl and ethyl parabens are toxic. They can cause contact dermatitis and other allergic reactions. Even worse, they can mimic the effects of estrogen, causing long-term damage to cells. They have also been shown in studies to release potentially cancer-causing chemicals. If it says paraben on the label, avoid it. They are used to inhibit microbial growth, which can be done more safely with grapefruit seed extract and other natural methods.

PVP/VA copolymer found in many hairsprays and cosmetics, may cause lung damage and ingestion may produce gas or kidney damage.

Petrolatum or mineral oil jelly can cause photosensitivity, meaning it promotes sun damage. It can interfere with the body's natural moisturizing ability. It also strips the natural oils of your skin causing dryness.

Artificial colors are generally labeled as FD&C or D&C followed by a number. Although the FDA approves them for use in drugs, cosmetics and sometimes food, most are toxic. Other approved dyes that should be avoided for your health and the environment are Azo dyes, which can cause tumors, nitro dyes, associated with liver damage and lack of oxygen in the blood, and quinolone, derived from coal tar, containing formaldehyde which is highly toxic and carcinogenic.

Artificial fragrances and cheap essential oils often cause allergic reactions and even lung damage.

TEA; triethanolamine and DEA; diethanolamine, used in brake fluid, anti freeze and industrial cleaners, and MEA and MIPA are found in shampoo, liquid soap, and conditioner. They can irritate the eyes and dry out skin and hair. When exposed to the air they form nitrosamines, which are toxic to the cardiovascular system, lungs, and digestive tract.

Stearalkonium chloride, used almost universally in hair conditioners, was developed as a fabric softener. Fine, if you consider your hair as a ball of yarn, but if you regard it as a protein growing out of living tissue, you will avoid it, as it can be toxic and cause allergic reactions.

Benzene, known to poison bone marrow, is a petrochemical widely used as a solvent in many personal care products. It is carcinogenic, mutagenic, changes genetic code, and can cause depression, convulsions, coma, and death. Vapors can be absorbed thru the skin and prolonged exposure is suspected of causing leukemia.

Steer clear!

ABOUT US

Together, we created Hair Mastery International, offering the world's most comprehensive and advanced trainings in holistic hair care and Hair Balancing since 1996. We offer workshops and seminars around the world, and at our permanent training location in Birch Bay, Washington. Hair Mastery International has set the standard for work with hair that emphasizes health and wellbeing for the client, the practitioner, and the planet. Our mission is to teach the highest standards and practices of holistic hair care with the Hair Balancing hair-cutting system and philosophy at its core. The precise way hair is cut and cared for has profound healing effects on the well being of both the client and practitioner. We are inspired to elevate hair care to a transformational healing experience, enhancing ease, life force, and fun.

With gratitude we share this ancient and new wisdom to co-create self-esteem, freedom, and beauty for all. We look forward to hearing from you.

www.hairmastery.com
info@hairmastery.com

Facebook
https://www.facebook.com/hairmastery

How Laura and Linda met

Mercury Yount, the originator of Hair Balancing, taught Laura this healing practice in the early 1980s. America was into perms and other chemical processes in that decade, so Mercury spent much more of his time in Europe, where the ultra-fine quality of his cutting technique was much appreciated. While working in Germany, Mercury met Linda who assisted him in many ways. He told her about Laura, who was still living and working in Los Angeles at the time. Years later, after Mercury's death, Linda moved to the US. Without a phone number or last name, she was unable to locate Laura. This was before the broad availability of the internet.

Later, when Linda was planning to move to LA from Hawaii, and was looking for a place to practice, she saw many ads for 'Office Space to Share.' One ad literally lit up. Linda called the number, and John Davis, Laura's husband, answered the phone. Linda described her space needs and John asked what work she would be doing there. Linda hesitated, not sure he would welcome a hair practitioner in a holistic healing office. John said he could not rent to her unless he knew what work she would be doing. Linda finally replied, "You have probably never heard of this work, ... it is called Hair Balancing." John asked, "Wouldn't you rather use the hair room?" Shocked, Linda answered, "You have a hair room?" And John said, "You'd better speak with my wife!"

When Linda called Laura in Birch Bay, Washington, they were delighted to discover their mutual connection to Mercury and that they would both be in California on the same days the following month. They arranged to meet and immediately felt a strong bond through Mercury and their experiences with Hair Balancing. In fact, they are convinced that Mercury orchestrated their meeting.

After balancing each others' hair and sharing all kinds of information and experiences, Laura and Linda created the Hair Mastery training. Laura and Linda continue to teach together and individually in both Europe and the United States, each adding their unique flavor and talents to the programs.

Laura Sullivan

My love of nature was kindled as I grew up exploring the forests, waters and wetlands around my home near Boston, Massachusetts. It has been a constant theme throughout my life, even the years I was in New York City. Living between Central Park and Riverside Park, I sought the trees, grass, and waters to ground me. My talents as a massage therapist funded my B.A. in Theatre, leading to a career in the entertainment industry including network television (ABC), writing, production, and acting. The latter brought me to LA, where I met Mercury Yount, the creator of Hair Balancing, at a Tantra workshop. He told me about his amazing way of cutting hair using Sacred Geometry, but I wasn't ready to experience it until a Beverly Hills hairdresser and his light body perm destroyed my long, straight, healthy hair. It was a life changing disaster. First of all, Hair Balancing healed me from that immediate hair trauma, and it also turned my straight hair into wash and wear, fabulous curls. Mercury was away more and more in Europe, and I wanted to keep my hair balanced, so I made sure to be in the only course he ever taught on how to do Hair Balancing. Looking at the diagrams of the system, I had the strange feeling that I had done this before. And although I only wanted to learn to maintain my own hair when he was away, I could not help but share this extraordinary healing art with friends. After Mercury's tragic passing, his clients sought me out, desperate to have their hair balanced. How could I refuse? And in truth, this healing art feeds my soul. I have loved all my varied careers, and yet the most fulfilling continues to be, practicing and teaching Hair Balancing and Holistic Hair Care. Nature continues to be my inspiration and teacher as I explore the best hair care possible for humans and our earth. It is a blessing to have been guided here, and it is my honor to share it with you. To learn more about Hair Balancing and details of my private practice, consult:

www.hairbalancingbylaura.com
agelesslaura@gmail.com

Linda Deslauriers

I was born and raised in Hamburg, Germany. As a teenager I experienced hair loss and other hair challenges. Back then you couldn't google; therefore a complex journey led me to my life long passion for classical homeopathy, Astrology, holistic health, psychology, and Hair Balancing. When I was seventeen, I started to practice yoga and meditation. Shortly thereafter I had a vision of a hair healer coming across the ocean. A few years later I met William Mercury Yount, who practiced and taught Hair Balancing. I spent hundreds of hours with him watching, translating, and learning but never intended to cut people's hair myself. However, when Mercury was traveling I started to help out his clients and began to balance their hair. After his sudden death in 1990 I knew that I had to continue and expand his legacy.

In 1991 I met the amazing pioneer in the magical world of hair, Anthony Morrocco. He shared with me his holistic hair care system, which uses astrologically based lunar cuts, Chinese medicine, chemical-free products, and proper hair and scalp care to promote healthy hair growth.

For my Master's in Clinical Psychology from the University of Hamburg I wrote a thesis on the significance of hair, and for my Master's in Literature from the University of Hawaii, I completed a thesis on hair symbolism in fairy tales. After yet another vision, in which I saw a comb carved out of rose quartz, I started to have Gemcombs made. You can find out more about them at www.gemcomb.com.

I am looking forward to hearing from you and feel honored to be of service and to share the profound and transformational teachings we have compiled. You can find my schedule at:

www.lindadeslauriers.com
linda@lindadeslauriers.com

Laura Sullivan & Linda Deslauriers

ACKNOWLEDGEMENTS

Photography & Graphic Design
Linda Deslauriers

Photo Credits
Baby Girl - Tiffany Nading
Stone Hearts, Cat & Aloe - Laura Sullivan
Lankauer Fire - Manfred Bohnhoff

Thank you to our models,
especially Shanti Deslauriers

Made in the USA
San Bernardino, CA
01 June 2016